OVERLORD
by Brian Jewell

the War Room handbook guide to the greatest military amphibious operation of all time...

6th June 1944

First published in Great Britain in 1994 by
The War Room
BROADWATER HOUSE
30 Park Parade
Harrogate, Yorkshire
HG1 5AG

© Brian Jewell, 1994
© for graphic design and cover
Meriel Yates and
Patrick Jewell, 1994

ISBN 0 9521009 5 9

Cataloguing in Publication data is
available from the British Library

AUTHOR'S NOTE

In this guide to OVERLORD, I have attempted to portray the magnitude of the operation and the topographical extent of the landing beaches. A recent visitor to the War Room told me he had attempted to cycle along the invasion beaches in a day but had had to give up! Military operations of the 1990s make headlines but are on a very small scale compared to those of the Second World War. This is because we live in a shrinking world, governed by cost-concious politicians, accountants and the Media. Modern weapons are more costly but less labour-intensive. Governments of major countries have to find salaries for their soldiers more in keeping with the remuneration that can be expected in civilian life.

We may well ask why men were willing to risk their lives for the pathetic ten shillings paid to the Infantryman of the 1940s as his weekly wage. Many, before the war, were used to working for a pittance; at least they were fed and clothed in the Armed Forces. It should also be remembered that the notion of a Patriotic Duty to fight for King and Country was generally accepted. This duty lay above all other considerations, and was the belief that had sustained the interests of Principalities and Powers for generations. In the United Kingdom, the myth was reinforced by a grandiose perception of Britain as the fountain-head of all that was noble in human society, a preposterous image swollen to monstrous proportions by Victorian Empire Builders.

Bravery in 1944 was taken for granted. It was not too difficult to put on a courageous front when all your mates were driven by the same impetus, and easier again if you were a Lance-Corporal Section Leader; even easier if you had the privilege of holding rank as a senior NCO. Better still if you held a commission: responsibility works wonders to create at least the semblance of fortitude.

Perhaps we shall never again see courage displayed on such a scale as at that best and worst of times. In 1944 on the beaches of Normandy, all were élite, not only Allied Servicemen. German troops, including conscripts from occupied countries, gave their all. A German presence in the D-Day ceremonies would not be inappropriate.

We must not forget those who took part in this, the greatest military operation of all time. Thank God their successors cannot be called upon to conduct themselves in such a way as was seen in 1944, except in a professional and better-paid capacity. When, in the course of duty, sensibilities are outraged, Counselling is now available, but in 1944, the word 'counsellling' in this context had not been invented. Even if it had been, the task of counselling the numbers involved would have been impossible. Could D-Day veterans be better-balanced had such therapy been available? Most old soldiers would be surprised at the suggestion.

What we commemorate on the 50th anniversary of D-Day are the bravery of the men who took part and the fact that D-Day was a mile post on the way towards the defeat of Fascism in Nazi Germany. The disturbing rise of neo-Fascism in Europe today must be regarded as a grave threat to that hard-won achievement.

Brian Jewell
The War Room
Harrogate
April 1994

CONTENTS

1	PRELUDE	*7*
2	BUILD-UP	*11*
3	WE'LL GO	*19*
4	THE BEACHES	*27*
5	BATTLE OF NORMANDY	*35*
6	THE COST	*43*
	APPENDICES	*45*

1 PRELUDE

Churchill called it 'Britain's finest hour', but for most of the population, including the troops who had been miraculously saved from the débâcle of Dunkirk, 1940 was a year of gloom. Alone, exhausted and daily expecting an invasion across the few brief miles of sea, it seemed to them inconceivable that one day the tides of war would turn and that from this island would be launched the greatest operation in military history. It cannot be too strongly emphasised that there never was, nor will be again, a campaign involving so many men as OVERLORD, but some four years were to pass before the great reverse could be launched.

The formation of the Commandos, whose first operation was on 22nd June 1940 - just two weeks after the British withdrawal from Dunkirk - gave a boost to morale at a time when it was most needed, although the reconnaissance raid they carried out on Boulogne on this date achieved little materially. Otherwise, 1940 was a time for licking wounds, and for turning the wheels of industry for the production of vital war materials.

Conscription had been introduced in 1938 and now each month or so brought call-up papers to men in further age groups.

At sea, Hitler's U-boats did their best to bring Britain to starvation but still the convoys came through, frequently battered and depleted.

'As England, in spite of her helpless military position, has shown herself unwilling to come to any compromise I have decided to begin preparations for, and if necessary to carry out, the invasion of England ... The English Air Force must be eliminated to such an extent that it will be incapable of putting up any substantial opposition to the invading troops.'

Thus spoke Adolf Hitler in June 1940, and so began what was to become known as the Battle of Britain. At that time Britain's fate lay in the hands of 1,243 men, the fighter pilots of the RAF.

All through that summer, the skies above South-East England were a battlefield with hundreds of aircraft engaged in dogfights. On Monday, 16th September, the *Daily Herald* carried as its lead story:

Goering's air force had lost 175 machines up to ten o'clock last night following a day which saw the fiercest air battles of the war. Fighters brought down 171 and AA fire 4.

Thirty British fighters were brought down, but ten of the pilots were safe.

This was a considerable exaggeration. The Luftwaffe losses were in fact 53 aircraft plus 16 damaged. The RAF lost 26 fighters with 13 pilots killed.

The Battle of Britain had been won by the Hurricanes and Spitfires of the Royal Air Force. Hitler was forced to abandon his plans for the invasion of this country, Operation SEA LION, and the air war was about to take a new form.

The air raid on London on the night of 25th/26th August 1940, marking the beginning of the Blitz, was carried out by German airmen contrary to the orders of higher command. Harried as they were by Anti-Aircraft guns and by RAF fighters, they abandoned their specified targets and haphazardly dropped their bombs wherever they could. Supposing that the raid was carried out in accordance with official German policy, RAF Bomber Command retaliated with a raid on Berlin.

On 6th September the Germans decided on a full-scale reprisal raid on London. The following afternoon, Reichmarshall Hermann Goering sent some 300 bombers escorted by 600 fighters across the Channel and the Londoners' ordeal by fire began. Before the end of the war eighteen thousand tons of high explosive and incendiary bombs were to fall on the nation's capital leaving an indelible memory on those who lived through it. But out of this suffering came remarkable spirit and courage, and for some, the Blitz brought a heightened sense of community and excitement.

Although raids continued spasmodically, the end of the Blitz 'proper' came for London on 10th May 1941, the night when the capital burned with over 2,000 fires and 1,436 people died. A quarter of a million books were burnt in the Library of the British Museum. Westminster Abbey, the Tower of London and the Royal Mint were also damaged.

This was the moment when Hitler turned his wrath towards the Russians and, just as the Blitz had ended the Battle of Britain, so the German invasion of Russia ended the Blitz.

In retrospect, 1941 can be seen as the year when the Axis powers over-reached themselves and started on the road to decline. On 2 June, Germany invaded the USSR in violation of the neutrality pact between them. At first the Red Army were forced back but they eventually sapped the aggressor's strength.

Later that year, on 7 December, the Japanese bombed the US naval base at Pearl Harbour, thus bringing the USA into the war against the Axis.

The resulting alliance of British-USSR-USA (in order of involvement) was a strange one, often with distrust and even positive dislike seething below the surface. The Summit Conferences, starting with Washington in December 1941, were very different from the images presented. Firstly, the British Prime Minister, Churchill, had no love for the Russian leader, Josef Stalin, and although there was an immediate need to eradicate the Nazi menace, Churchill made no secret of the fact that he felt the further east the Russians were kept, the better. To this end, he favoured a drive up through Italy or the

Balkans when the time came to invade Europe. There was also a little matter of the non-aggression pact that had existed between Germany and Russia, at the time when Britain stood alone. Roosevelt, the US President, on the other hand, felt in some ways more in harmony with Stalin, having a common dislike of British Imperialism. He also shared the Russian's view that the invasion of Europe should come from the west. Stalin's demands were simple and direct - he wanted a Second Front in the west and wanted it now to relieve the pressure on his own country and, at the same time, called for arms and material supplies which could be ill-afforded by Britain.

In the event, Stalin and Roosevelt had much their own way; but the invasion was not to come as early as they would have liked. Stalin wanted it then, in 1941, and Roosevelt aimed at an invasion of France in the autumn of 1942. Both the dates were quite impracticable. In no way could sufficient build-up of forces and equipment be made in the available time.

War indeed makes for strange bedfellows!

Despite the undeniable courage of the bomber crews, the air war was not a completely glorious record. Too many beautiful cities both on the mainland of Europe and in England were devastated by bombing, often without justifiable cause, and sometimes under the excuse of retaliation.

Such is the organised vandalism of war.

2 BUILD-UP

'We are not allies. We have plenty of allies among the United Nations, but we who are to undertake this great operation are one indivisible force.'

General Eisenhower to his staff,
December 1943.

In his book *Normandy to the Baltic,* Field Marshal Montgomery described the object of OVERLORD thus:

To mount and carry out an operation, with forces and equipment established in the United Kingdom and with target date 1st May 1944, to secure a lodgement on the Continent from which further offensive operations could be developed. The lodgement area must contain sufficient port facilities to maintain a force of some twenty-six to thirty divisions and enable that force to be augmented by follow-up shipments from the United States or elsewhere of additional divisions and supporting units at the rate of three to five divisions per month.

This was the essence of the Grand Plan that had been evolved in 1942 by a planning team under the direction of the British Lieutenant-General Sir Frederick Morgan who held the newly-created position of Chief of Staff to the Supreme Allied Commander (COSSAC).

By common consent, the Supreme Commander of OVERLORD would be an American. The man selected was General Dwight D. Eisenhower who was US Commander in North Africa: it was there that he met the General who was to be his Commander of Ground Forces, Sir Bernard Law Montgomery. On New Year's Eve 1943, the two men met at Marrakesh and first saw the COSSAC plan for OVERLORD.

The choice of Normandy for Allied landings, between the Cotentin peninsular and the Bay of the Seine, was influenced by several considerations. Initially, the coast around Calais seemed to be a suitable location because of its short distance from England in terms of sea miles and flying time. But the Germans could also see the sense of this choice and had amassed considerable forces in the area.

The alternatives were to look at the north and to the south-west. The north, in Flanders, was dismissed as the ground was too vulnerable to defence flooding. That left the south-west, the area eventually selected. It had several advantages; it was, in part, sheltered from Atlantic gales by the Cotentin peninsula, and there was the nearby port of Cherbourg for supplying the forces; there was also the bonus that the area could be cut off from German reinforcements in the east, simply by bombing the thirty-odd bridges over the Seine.

Thus the scene was set, and the build-up for OVERLORD began. Through the Spring of 1944 the Allied forces were training and preparing for D-Day and there was an increasing awareness that the offensive could only be weeks away.

The beaches chosen for the OVERLORD landings are wide and sandy. Behind them are drained salt marshes or sand-dunes. Only between the Vire and the town of Arromanches, a distance of some 20 miles, are there cliffs with sheer 100-foot drops into the sea. But these cliffs are broken in two places: by the harbour of Port-en-Bessin and by the beach of Vierville. Here, the Americans were to make one of their two landings, code-named OMAHA.

Inland there is the *bocage*, a Norman word meaning 'copse'. It is a countryside of hedges on earth banks enclosing irregularly-shaped fields. The twenty miles of cliff and the *bocage* gave some natural advantages to the defenders, particularly the *bocage* which was to prove an expensive obstacle to the Allies attempting to break out of the bridgehead.

Generalfeldmarschall Erwin Rommel returned to Europe from North Africa late in 1943, at first to command an Army Group in Bavaria and Northern Italy. He was soon given the task of inspecting the coastal defences of what the Germans called the Atlantic Wall. What he found was alarming; for the most part defences were non-existent. Admittedly, around the large ports there were heavy guns and forces of troops for their protection, but elsewhere the Wall comprised only a few mines and strands of barbed wire.

In his attempts to improve the position, Rommel applied for and was granted the command of Army Group B - the German Armies stationed between the Netherlands and the Loire, directly subordinate to Generalfeldmarschall von Rundstedt commanding Army Group West.

Rommel predicted that the Allied attack, when it came, would be launched against that part of the French coast around the mouth of the Somme. It was in this area, as well as in Normandy, that he decided to concentrate efforts to build up defences.

The 'Wall' that Rommel quickly effected was intended to stop the invaders on the beaches. In the tidal area there were driven huge beams inclined towards the sea, and tipped with steel spikes to hole landing craft or with mines. In the sea itself concrete obstructions were built with naval mines anchored in the shallow water. 'Element C' was a mixed bag of tricks with fences of iron and ferro-concrete erections, all intended to blow up or impede the progress of invading men and vehicles. Of course, there were the conventional minefields and the beach areas covered by a miscellany of armaments encased in concrete bunkers.

Off the beaches, defenders were holed up in deep entrenchments, and possible landing fields sprouted 'Rommel's asparagus' - heavy posts intended to wreck the Allied gliders, when they landed.

When the invasion came, Rommel's defensive preparations were only about twenty per cent completed.

Certainly, the French Resistance was of considerable help to the Allies at the time of the Normandy landings, but its effectiveness depended on arms, equipment and guidance provided from across the Channel. The British Government had been encouraging and fostering the Resistance since the débâcle of 1940. It had to be a softly-softly enterprise as any large-scale organisation would have laid itself open to discovery by the Gestapo, with brutal reprisals.

The operation from London consisted of the dropping by parachute and landing by Lysander aircraft of specialist agents to contact the Resistance and advise on subversive activities that would have the greatest effect. The agents' brief was a roaming one with no fixed territories, and instructions to avoid political affiliations and not to attempt to form chains of command and subordination.

Many agents were French citizens who were brought out of occupied France, trained in Britain, and returned to the continent. On D-Day there were some 300 such agents working with the French Resistance. Their duty had been hazardous during the occupation years; there were 64 known Gestapo victims and no fewer than 297 of their number simply disappeared.

Through the months leading up to D-Day a number of secret forays were made on the invasion coast by members of 2 Special Boat Squadron - the Royal Naval equivalent to the Army's Special Air Service (SAS) and by men from three (Miscellaneous) Troops, 10 (Inter-Allied) Commando. These activities provided invaluable information on the German shore defences.

As D-Day approached so Resistance activities were accelerated, with sabotage of railways, telephone services, and ambush of German road transport. Other important Resistance work was the demolition or neutralising of electrical generating plants and factories in production for the Germans.

In the three months before D-Day, 1,500 tons of equipment and arms were air-dropped into France, in addition to about 150 men; from D-Day until the end of August 1944, these numbers were increased to 6,500 and 400 respectively.

Added to this support for the Resistance, the Allies, during OVERLORD, introduced other means of assistance: the 'Jedburgh' teams, small groups of French, British and American personnel to guide air drop supplies behind the German lines, where and when needed. The other back-up was provided by the Special Air Service task forces, some 1,900 British and French officers and men who were parachuted in to carry out specific tasks.

Operation NEPTUNE, the Naval part of OVERLORD, comprised two Task Forces: 'West' to land and support the US land forces on OMAHA and UTAH beaches, and 'East' for the British beaches of GOLD, JUNO and SWORD.

Every beach was allocated a Force Headquartership, and every Beach Force was known by an appropriate letter: Force O, Force U, Force G, Force J and Force S.

Apart from these Assault Forces, there was also a Naval Bombarding Force for each sector.

American troops for the D-Day landings were mainly assembled in the West of England, whereas the British and Canadians assembled around Southampton and eastward.

As each ship was loaded with heavy stores, it moved out to anchor offshore to await the final assembly for the Channel crossing.

The American Ninth Air Force and the British 2nd Tactical Air Force had been formed and equipped for the cover and support of the Naval and ground forces engaged in OVERLORD. But Eisenhower needed something more to attack the communication links between Germany and France. In the

Spring of 1944, he succeeded in having both the US Eighth and Ninth Air Forces and RAF Bomber Command seconded to his control. The Allied Air Forces had been engaged in bombing German industrial targets and now, in their new role, were highly sucessful in attacking the railways linking France with Germany. During their operations, over 1,500 French railway engines were destroyed, a considerable contribution to keeping down the number of German troops in Normandy.

Other targets for Bomber Command and the US Air Forces were the road bridges over the river Seine. In this they were, to all practical purposes, completely successful.

An essential element in the invasion of Normandy was deception. Plans were evolved aimed at persuading the Germans to believe that the main invasion would take place on other parts of the occupied coastline. There were two parts to the Allied deception plan. The first, codenamed FORTITUDE NORTH was intended to convey to the enemy that the invasion would be directed at the occupying forces in Norway. The second, FORTITUDE SOUTH, fostered the belief that a massive attack would be forced across the narrow Straits of Dover in the Pas de Calais area. RAF and USAAF aircraft struck at targets in the area and in Britain a complex programme of 'now you see it - now you don't' illusion was enacted. From the air, enemy reconnaissance planes could see what appeared to be landing craft on the Rivers Thames and Medway but were in fact no more than cardboard and plywood imitations. Dummy gliders were dispersed in Kentish airfields, and inflatable rubber and canvas tanks and trucks lined leafy lanes. A vast volume of fake wireless traffic representing troop movements was transmitted from vans travelling around the Home Counties. General George S. Patton's Third US Army, which was to be used as the main American follow-up force in Normandy, was supposedly based in the South-East to add to the general illusion, whereas, in reality, the main part of the Third Army was 150 miles away in Cheshire. The FORTITUDE operations were a great success, keeping valuable German armour and infantry tied up in the

Pas de Calais area for some weeks after the Normandy invasion had taken place.

As early as February 1944, the British Isles were virtually sealed from the rest of the world, particularly from neutral countries where German Intelligence abounded. Then in April, a strip of coast ten miles deep, all the way round from the Wash to Lands End, was closed to visitors. Postal and telephone services were severely cut and any overseas mail censored.

In May at ports all over the country, merchant ships and Naval landing craft were loaded with the hardware needed for this massive amphibious operation.

The success of OVERLORD and the lives of thousands of men depended on maintaining the strictest possible security. The issue of plans and orders for the invasion was kept to the minimum, those in circulation being codenamed BIGOT, a classification above 'Top Secret'. People cleared to receive them were described as 'Bigoted'.

As time for the invasion approached, the troops who were to take part were 'sealed' in embarkation camps which meant that apart from being confined within barbed wire barriers and fences, they were not permitted to send letters or to make telephone calls.

An advance of £1 or so in French francs was issued as was a gilt-coloured tin of emergency food - a chocolate flavoured compound that swelled when eaten, taking away the pangs of hunger. There were instructions on the tin to the effect that it should only be eaten in dire circumstances and then only one square every few hours. It was rumoured that if the instructions were not observed to the letter the stomach would expand to an irreparable extent!

D-Day was to have been Monday 5 June, but on the Saturday before, the weather broke causing another day's wait in the embarkation camps or afloat for those unlucky enough to have been taken aboard.

One soldier remembers:

The evening before we embarked I took a walk through the vehicle lines, devoid of human attendance.

It would have been good to have gone out to a pub for a final drink before leaving England's shore, but we were not allowed beyond the area.

A barrage balloon flopped around about 100 feet above the ground, and the DD Shermans and a couple of jeeps stood immobile in the fading light, as if they had been there for years instead of a few days.

I climbed on to one of the tanks and wondered what would be its fate. Perhaps it might even survive for a victory parade through some German city.

3 'WE'LL GO'

The fighting ships had begun to move south from their northern bases on 2 June. The following day the convoys which had been assembling off Falmouth sailed for the east.

All was prepared for D-Day on the 5th. However, in the small hours of the 4th, Eisenhower had been given a meteorological report forecasting very bad weather, probably lasting for the next three days. At dawn he decided to postpone the venture for 24 hours and ordered the vessels already at sea to return. In fact, some ships and craft destined for UTAH beach in the American landing sector of FORCE U could not be contacted by wireless signal and destroyers had to be sent to bring them back.

Sunday, 4 June, was a stormy day and fears grew that it might not be possible to carry out the invasion in the few days when the tides would be right. In the evening, the Supreme Commander learned from his RAF Metereological Officer Group Captain J. M. Stagg that there was a slim chance of better weather lasting until the evening of the 6th.

The fate of the entire operation was in the balance and Eisenhower had to make one of the most dangerous decisions in military history. By dawn on the 5th he had made up his mind. It was 'We'll go' and the ships were again on the move.

OVERLORD had begun in earnest.

The sheer size of the Operation NEPTUNE, the seaborne part of OVERLORD, defies the imagination. A total of 6,939 ships were engaged in the crossing, the number made up by 1,213 Naval Fighting Ships, 4,126 Landing Ships and Craft, 736 Ancillary Ships and Craft, 864 Merchant Ships. Fifty-four small craft, including 20 Rhino ferries or towing craft were lost in the crossing.

It was a near miracle that out of all these vessels the great majority reached the French coast at all, let alone the achievement of arriving at their allotted time, almost to the minute.

It was a moment of great apprehension and illogical surmise. A typical feeling at the time was:

I admit I was scared and seasick on the way over. What the hell would be waiting for us? I kept thinking - 'Well, the Army feeds us at regular intervals, and the way to face this is to take the intervals between meals as those of danger ... Get through the time between breakfast and lunch and lunch and the evening meal, and I'll be alright'.

In the event, of course, meals did not come at regular intervals and there was that terrible moment on the third day when almost all the platoon were wiped out by a mortar shell while scoffing Maconochies (tinned meat and vegetable stew), *before starting on the treacle pudding.*

The minesweepers were in sight of the French coast early in the evening of the 5th, their sweeping duty taking them sufficiently close to shore to recognise houses, but the Germans ignored them.

German Naval S Boats - fast torpedo vessels - did not appear at this time and were presumably tied up in the harbours of Cherbourg and Le Havre.

The 82nd and 101st US Airborne Divisions, commanded by Major General Matthew B. Ridgway and Major General Maxwell Taylor respectively, had been ordered to drop on the Cotentin peninsular to support the landings on UTAH beach.

It was by no means a universally approved plan and some officers on the SHEAF staff had misgivings. The ground for the proposed drop had been flooded as part of Rommel's Atlantic Wall defences, fields which were still dry were mined and, equally bad, the Anti-Aircraft defences were particularly strong in the area.

Of the two divisions, the 82nd was the only one to have been in previous action and had had a particularly rough time supporting the Sicilian landings at Salerno, whereas the 101st had been raised for D-Day and would be going into action for the first time.

About midnight on 2 June, two Royal Navy midget submarines, X20 and X23, left Portsmouth for the French coast, their mission to act as markers showing flashing green beacons off JUNO and SWORD beaches respectively. These submarine craft each carried a crew of two Naval Lieutenants and an engine room artificer, augmented by a Combined Operations pilotage-party of two Naval officers.

For the first part of their voyage they were towed by trawlers but for most of the passage they were unescorted. After identifying the two beaches, they were to submerge and remain hidden. On the morning of D-Day, in darkness, they were to surface and show their beacons as guides for the assault landing craft. The darkness meant any distinguishing features on the shore were hard to identify, but the task was vital because of the dangerous outcrop of rock in a number of places, and the mud flats where the Orne flows into the sea.

The midget submarines reached the French coast shortly before dawn on Sunday, 4 June, and lay on the bottom until light, when they surfaced to periscope depth in order to take bearings on the shore. Having done so and noting no signs of movement, they anchored and submerged again where they remained for the rest of the day and through the daylight hours of the 5th.

It was at 0508 hours on the 6th that X23 lit her beacon off SWORD beach, closely followed by X20 at JUNO. X23's log read:

'0500, surfaced and checked position by shore fix in dawn light. Rigged mast with lamp and radar beacon.'

This was seventy-six hours after leaving Portsmouth, sixty-four of which had been spent under water, a remarkable test of endurance for the five men in each craft in their extremely cramped conditions.

The Germans undoubtedly felt safe that night, convinced that no invasion force would be capable or mad enough to go to sea in such heavy weather. Rommel, commanding Army Group B, had even decided to make a quick visit to Germany to celebrate his wife's birthday.

There was, of course, the drone from the engines of the bombers of the RAF and the USAAF, but there was nothing unusual in that - they had been attacking coastal and inland targets for months.

The brief of the 82nd US Airborne Division was to isolate the western flank of the invasion area by taking the crossroads at Ste-Mère-Eglise and by capturing or destroying bridges over the rivers Merderet and Douve. The task of their compatriots in the 101st was to take the town of Carentan and keep open the landward roads for the seaborne forces.

Horsa troop-carrying glider

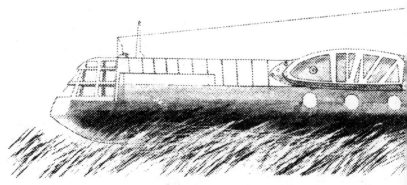

Pathfinders of the American Airborne Divisions took off two hours before midnight on the 5th. Because of low cloud over Normandy the aircraft navigators were unable to visually check their positions and in consequence, the pathfinders parachuted some way off their planned Dropping Zones, and had to set up their Eureka radio beacons and lights where they landed. Unfortunately, the same navigational problem beset the main airborne force resulting in confusion of regiments landing in the wrong DZs. Other parachutists were scattered over an area of several hundred square miles.

However, all was not lost and everywhere the airborne men were fighting battles as individuals or in small groups, eventually linking up into larger groups and achieving most of their original objectives, one of which was the town of Ste-Mère-Eglise, which was taken at approximately 0400 hours, on the 6th. The cost was high: around 20 per cent casualties.

The British 6th Airborne Division, commanded by Major General Sir Richard Gale, was given the task of taking or destroying the bridges on the eastern flank of the beaches, on the high ground between the rivers Orne and Dives. In particular two bridges over the Orne and the Caen Canal had to be captured before the Germans could destroy them.

In the first few minutes of D-Day, gliders carrying men of the 2nd Battalion Oxfordshire and Buckinghamshire Light Infantry and Sappers under the command of Major John Howard, crash-landed in a field close to the bridge, breaking the wings off the gliders on Rommel's 'asparagus posts' as they did so. The Major's glider came to rest a bare fifty yards from the Canal Bridge closely followed by two other gliders of his force. Completely surprised, the German defenders of the bridge were overwhelmed and the bridge taken and held despite German counter-attacks. This was to become known as Pegasus Bridge, after the Airborne forces' insignia emblem, and it was here, in the afternoon of D-Day that men of the 1st Special Service Brigade, led by Bill Millin, the personal piper of the commander, Lord Lovat, joined up with Major Howard's tired but successful force.

Another major objective for the 6th Airborne Division was the silencing of a well-defended German coastal artillery battery at Merville. The task was allocated to Lieutenant Colonel Terence Otway of the 9th Parachute Regiment who devised a dangerous plan involving bombing by the RAF, storming of the battery by paratroopers, a simultaneous glider landing, and a bombardment from warships off-shore. The complex plan broke down in the confusion of the overall operation. However at 0430 hours the airborne men attacked the guns, silencing them for D-Day, but at the cost of nearly fifty per cent casualties.

Like the situation in the American Zones, things went wrong for the British paratroops, bad drops resulting in men being scattered over wide areas. However, most objectives were achieved, albeit at substantial cost.

Assault by glider on the Caen Canal and Orne River bridges by six platoons of the 2nd Ox & Bucks Light Infantry and thirty sappers from 249 Company RE. The glider of Major John Howard, leading the assault, landed within 50 yards of the canal bridge (left) in the first few minutes of D-Day. >

4 THE BEACHES

'Believe me, Lang, the first 24 hours of the invasion will be decisive ... for the Allies, as well as for Germany, it will be the longest day!'

Rommel to his aide-de-camp,
April 1944

The troopships had been arriving at their assembly points since midnight, and everything was going according to plan despite the heavy seas.

The landing craft left the main fleet to head for the beaches. From the craft, amphibious tanks were launched, but some of them were swamped before reaching the shore.

The Bombarding Forces of Operation NEPTUNE were, with the bombing by the combined Allied Air Forces, intended to soften up the German defences prior to the landings of assault troops. The western beaches UTAH and OMAHA were assigned to Western Task Force, commanded by Rear-Admiral A. G. Kirk aboard the Task flagship USS *Augusta*.

Bombardment Force A had responsibility for UTAH beach, with a complement of 16 ships, including the USS *Nevada*, and USS *Tuscaloosa*, flagship of Force A.

On the left, Bombardment Force C, with sights set on OMAHA beach, was headed by the battleships USS *Texas* (flagship) and USS *Arkansas*. Their strength was supplemented by 3 cruisers and 11 destroyers.

GOLD, JUNO and SWORD beaches were the responsibility of Eastern Task Force, under the command of Rear-Admiral Sir Philip Vian, in the cruiser HMS *Scylla*. GOLD and JUNO beaches came under the guns of Bombarding Forces K and E respectively. The 18 ships that were assigned to GOLD and 13 to JUNO were mainly destroyers. SWORD beach, however, had the larger Bombardment Force D allocated to it. The destroyer section alone was 13 in number, and their part in the bombardment took place with the ships only a few hundred yards off the shore. Flagships for the Eastern Bombarding Task Force were HMS *Belfast* (Force E), HMS *Mauritius* (Force D) and HMS *Argonaut* (Force K).

In addition to all these regular warships, both task forces had their own reserves, mainly destroyers drawn from escort duty, and as a General Reserve there was the battleship HMS *Nelson.*

Besides these Bombarding Forces, each Assault Force had further backing from an assortment of landing craft specially equipped with various close support weapons.

Before the landings, the Bombarding Forces had to rely on direct and aircraft observation for reporting the accuracy of the attack. This was provided by four squadrons of Fleet Air Arm Seafires, five RAF squadrons of Spitfires and Mustangs and US Navy pilots flying 15 Spitfires. Seven aircraft were lost in this part of the operation. When the troops were ashore, the air observation was supplemented by FOB (Forward Observation Bombardment) units, made up of Naval officers and signallers with radio sets.

The heavy air attack that complemented the bombardment from the sea involved the night raiding by the planes from RAF Bomber Command and some sixteen hundred bombing aircraft of the US 8th and 9th Air Forces. On UTAH beach, the final bombing by 269 low flying Marauders took place only ten minutes before the landing of the troops and was generally successful.

On OMAHA and on the British front the situation was complicated by poor visibility and the bombers had to use the alternative plan of flying in line-abreast formation and bombing under the orders of pathfinders. OMAHA was attacked by 329 high flying Liberators, which, because of low cloud, ran the risk of bombing incoming landing craft. In consequence, bombs were dropped well off target and were scattered up to three miles inland.

The coastal air bombardment overall was perhaps only partially successful but it had the effect of keeping the defending German troops under cover until 10 minutes before H-Hour.

The assault on UTAH beach in the American sector was the responsibility of the 4th Infantry Division of VII Corps, commanded by Major-General J. L. Collins, carried in 865 ships and craft provided and commanded by Rear Admiral Don P. Moon, United States Navy.

The Task Force arrived at the assembly area off UTAH beach at 0200 hours on the 6th after a stormy crossing with plenty of seasickness amoung the troops. First ashore was a contingent of 124 men of the US Cavalry, landing on the small offshore Iles de Marcouf which were void of the enemy. As the troops moved into the assault landing craft, the beach was being bombarded by Marauders of the Ninth US Air Force and from the sea by the Naval Task Force. Along with the troops went the close support landing craft equipped with guns and thirty-two DD tanks provided by the British 79th Armoured Division - of which twenty-eight managed to make the landing.

However, it was by no means a smooth and uneventful operation; the 8th Regimental Combat Team found themselves ashore, certainly, but something like a mile off their target. The situation was righted by some remarkable leadership on the part of Brigadier-General Theodore Roosevelt, attached to the US 4th Division who marshalled troops from the beach. Regrettably, a few days later the General was to die from a heart attack.

UTAH was not an easy landing but by the afternoon and early evening the 4th Division was pushing inland and joining up with the US paratroops who had landed on the previous night.

One of the most adventurous landing actions was that of three companies of the US Provisional Ranger Force (the US equivalent to British Commandos) commanded by Lt Col James E. Rudder, whose task was to neutralise the heavy artillery battery at Pointe du Hoc jutting out into the Bay of the Seine on the Calvados coast.

The Rangers' attack had to be made up the sheer 100 foot cliff which had been given a liberal dressing of barbed wire and trip flares. Back in Britain, Lt Col Rudder had decided on a frontal storm up the cliff with mortar-fired grappling lines, scaling ladders and some fire-escapes supplied by the National Fire Service, and had been exercising the Rangers on the cliffs of the Isle of Wight.

On the day, the assault landing craft carrying the Rangers were spotted by the Germans and shelled by the guns on the shore. But with supporting fire from their escorting destroyer, a landing was made and lines shot up the cliffs by the mortars. The ascent was made but by this time the Germans had withdrawn the guns to positions some half a mile inland. Eventually, the guns were destroyed but the Germans counter-attacked. The Rangers were under siege for two days and were later relieved by some of the second wave troops from OMAHA beach.

Aboard the USS *Augusta* at 1000 hours on D-Day, there was concern. General Omar Bradley, in charge of the American land forces, had good news from UTAH beach. Although there had been considerable resistance, the objectives must have been gained by the Airborne troops as the UTAH forces were finding their way through the beach exits.. As the guns on the Pointe du Hoc were now silent, it was reasonable to suppose that the Rangers had done their job. But from OMAHA beach there was nothing but bad news. Reports from General Gerow, the Corps Commander, spoke of heavy casualties and heavy losses of DD Tanks, intensive artillery and machine-gun fire.

OMAHA was better protected by the Germans than any other invasion beach. To them it had seemed an obvious place for a landing. The initial occupation of this beach had been entrusted to the 1st Infantry Division commanded by Major-General Clarence R. Huebner. In the following wave came the 29th Infantry Division.

The causes behind the trouble were complex: firstly, the invading force was not strong enough to beat the defenders. Secondly, the assembly area where the troops were to tranship into their assault craft, and where the DD Tanks were to take to the water, was all of 12 miles from the landing; the sea was rough and many of the craft and tanks were swamped - twenty-seven of the DDs being lost with most of their crews, and the majority of the troops were suffering from sea-sickness. Most of the beach obstacles were under water and these took heavy toll of the craft and troops.

By noon the position was such that Bradley was considering the evacuation of OMAHA and ordering his follow-up forces to land at either UTAH or the British beaches, when came the message 'advancing up heights.'

The men of the 1st US Infantry Division (the 'Big Red One' which was returning to French soil for the first time since the First World War) were tired of being pinned down and slowly, with losses at every step, they were getting off the beach. To the right, the 29th Division was now ashore and taking heavy punishment, but like the 1st they were also making slow progress inland.

Because of differences in times of tide the British and Canadian Armies landed on their respective beaches half an hour after the American assault. The Naval Bombardment had done a good job and the troops were able to gain a foothold. However, the German resistance was fierce and as the area was comparatively built-up, street-fighting, that slow, slogging style of warfare, was inevitable.

On GOLD beach the 50th (Northumbrian) Division had the task of pushing inland between La Rivière and Le Hamel and of taking Arromanches and Bayeux. The Division's 69th and 231st Brigades landed at La Rivière and Le Hamel respectively and found themselves heavily engaged by troops of the German 352nd Division, the same force that was giving so much trouble to the Americans on OMAHA. It was the specialised armour, the 'funnies' of the 79th Armoured Division 'zoo' that greatly helped the British troops to get off the beach but not without heavy casualties. In addition, the use of 'Bangalore Torpedoes' was helping clear the beach of obstructions. The 'Bangalore Torpedo' was a simple but affective device for destroying barbed-wire defences. A length of metal tubing was filled with explosive and a short Time Fuse was inserted at one end. Two soldiers ran up to the wire carrying the torpedo which was then pushed through the entanglement and the fuse lit after which the men retired to a 'safe' distance.

The No. 47 (Royal Marine) Commando had a particularly arduous task although they came ashore two hours after the first landing. Their target was Port-en-Bessin, a small port on the right extremity of GOLD beach. The idea was to attack the port from the land side and, in order to do this, the Commando would have a ten mile march. Unfortunately when the Commando came ashore they found that the assault troops, in this case the 1st Hampshires, were having a bad time, losing their commanding officer and many others of their strength in the engagement. The 47 Commando did not reach Port-en-Bessin before dark on the 6th and it took another day to capture the town.

To return to the fortunes of the 50th Division. At La Rivière the 69th Brigade landed and advanced inland. One company of the 5th Battalion East Yorkshire Regiment was, however, pinned down on the beach and again the assault troops had reason to thank the specialised armour of the 79th for relieving their plight. Similar incidents, great and small, were happening on GOLD throughout the 6th, but by the end of the day the beach was firmly held and the 50th Division, by now well inland, had linked with the Canadians who had landed at JUNO. These were the 3rd Canadian Division and the 2nd Canadian Armoured Brigade. Their aim was to advance inland from the beach and take Carpiquet airfield near Caen. Of course, this was vital if General Montgomery's intention to capture Caen by the evening of the first day was to be realised. In the event, it was not to be until 10 July that Caen would be 'neutralised', and the 18th before all the suburbs were eventually cleared of the enemy.

The Canadians did not have a good start to their day; many of their landing craft were wrecked or blown up on the obstructions and, as they had been delayed by bad weather, the beach at high tide was too narrow for the adequate marshalling of their equipment.

On JUNO beach, as on GOLD, the specialised armour of the 79th gave valuable help to the troops in getting off the beach.

Canadian tanks had, by the afternoon, cut the Caen-Bayeux road seven miles inland and it seemed that Caen itself by nightfall might yet be possible. But the Germans counter-attacked, thus delaying the impetus and allowing further German reinforcements in the area, and Caen did not fall.

Between the Canadians on JUNO and the British 3rd Division eastward on SWORD was an area allotted to two Royal Marine Commandos: the 41st and the 48th. The brief of the latter was to land at the small village of St Aubin two hours after the Canadians had made their assault on JUNO, and at the same time 41 (Royal Marine) Commando was to land five miles eastward at Lion-sur-Mer. The two were then to turn to each other and meet, mopping up the enemy positions as they went. However, events were not to turn out that way; the 49th not only came under unexpectedly heavy attack from German artillery but their strength was greatly depleted by the loss of some landing craft, with those rescued finding themselves on a return voyage to England. The 41st at Lion-sur-Mer also had some troubles but the main difficulty came when darkness fell and a mixed force of armour and infantry of the 21st Panzer Division succeeded in reaching the coast at Luc-sur-Mer, between the two Commandos, thus splitting the British and Canadian beaches. However, this threat was not to last, the Germans withdrawing as follow-up landings progressed.

The most easterly of the invasion beaches was SWORD with the British 3rd Division landing at La Brèche. This was a built-up area and the Germans had taken the opportunity of converting the houses into defensive bunkers. This was the only area where the Allies met German Naval opposition in the shape of three S Boats - in this action the Norwegian destroyer *Svenner* was torpedoed and sunk.

The landing was expensive in terms of casualties and equipment but by 0900 hours La Brèche had been taken and an advance made inland towards Coleville.

Finally, the town of Ouistreham on the eastern extremity of SWORD had to be taken and this was achieved in the early afternoon by No. 4 Commando and two troops of French Commandos. The French Commando troops at Ouistreham were led by Captain Philippe Keiffer who had his son and daughter in Paris and therefore a special personal reason to see that the Allies were quickly off the beaches and on their way to the French capital. Unfortunately for Keiffer his son was killed fighting for the Resistance before Paris could be reached.

D-Day ended and history had been made; many gallant men of the total of nearly 133,000 put ashore in seventeen hours had died but the number was less than expected. To all who took part it was a momentous day; they would never, could never, see its like again.

5 BATTLE OF NORMANDY

'As a result of the D-Day operations, a foothold has been gained on the continent of Europe.'

General Sir Bernard Montgomery's report,
6 June, 1944

As the beach-head was strengthened and the battle moved slowly inland, life close to the landing areas took on a kind of routine. A sapper who had landed at GOLD beach remembers a moment of 'normality':

'It must have been the second or third evening after the landing that we were given an hour or two of relaxation with a session of Housey-Housey in a mess tent erected in a field alongside an orchard. This was a game now universally known as Bingo and was probably the only gambling permitted in the British Army.

Our CSM was the caller and his shouts of "legs eleven" and "ducks on a pond" had a strange ring of reassurance in this alien place. We were much more used to him calling out "That man there!" or "I'm standing on what's supposed to be your short and curlies!"

But the memory of that evening, on which we were given our first ration of beer, is of the wasps from the orchard, and going back to the tin mug after an "eyes down" to find five or six wasps floating in the beer.'

Among the first vehicles to come ashore were jeeps fitted as ambulances. These were part of the services for the wounded that ranged from Field Ambulance units and Advanced Field Dressing Stations, as part of each formation, to complete Field Hospitals which were established as the beach-head was strengthened.

The work of the medical orderlies and stretcher bearers at company level was impressive. In the thick of battle, under cover of a white flag with a red cross, white helmets and armbands, these men went about tending friend and foe alike and removing them to the Royal Army Medical Corps doctors at the Advanced Field Dressing Stations.

It was not uncommon to see British or American medical staff working with their German counterparts, who had come in as prisoners. Of course, casualties were inevitable but it is fair to say that both sides generally respected the sign of the red cross and the non-combatant status of those who wore it.

The MULBERRY harbour design and provision had been the responsibility of the Royal Navy. These artificial harbours, originally suggested by Winston Churchill, had been undergoing construction throughout 1943.

Two complete harbours were required, one for OMAHA and the other for GOLD off Arromanches. The outer breakwaters, known as GOOSEBERRIES were, in fact, merchant ships deliberately scuttled and sunk so as to provide calm waters within the harbour. The piers, or unloading roadways, floated and went up and down with the tide.

160 tugs and 10,000 men were needed to assemble the two harbours at their locations. Unfortunately, the OMAHA MULBERRY was only to be operated for a few days, becoming wrecked in a gale that started on 19 June.

The GOLD MULBERRY, however, continued in service for many months, and the Americans found they could quite satisfactorily beach cargo ships on UTAH for unloading trucks.

The battle for Villers-Bocage was typical of actions in the early days of the invasion.

Men of the 7th Armoured Division - the 'Desert Rats' - had just occupied the small town of some 1,000 inhabitants when the

Germans opened fire. The British tanks in the lanes up to the town were 'hull-down' behind hedges but each time they moved they were fired on. The action was going badly for the British and those in the town were compelled to withdraw, leaving a squadron of tanks outflanked by the enemy infantry.

Fire was coming from all directions and German anti-tank 88mm guns made sure that an English tank could turn a corner only at its peril. As reported by War Correspondent Alan Moorehead, in his excellent account of the campaign, *Eclipse:*

'At this stage the Germans were far ahead of us in using the country. Their infantry smothered themselves in leaves and branches. They crawled up to the forward positions on their stomachs. They never showed themselves. Whole platoons of soldiers would lie themselves into the leafy branches of trees, and there they would wait silently for hours, even days, until they got the chance of a shot ... You had to be ready to jump for the ditches at every daylight hour ...'

At last it was decided that Villers-Bocage should be bombed, and bombed it was: twenty minutes of hell made it a ruinous pile of bricks. Again the British troops went forward, only to be met by the same opposition - the Germans had simply taken to the fields when the air raid started! The devastation was in vain, and it was to be days before the town was eventually retaken.

From the Allies' viewpoint, actions such as Villers-Bocage were the negative side of June 1944, before the inevitable breakthrough.

Over 2,000 tons of bombs fell on Caen prior to the attack of the Allied ground forces.

At 0430 hours on 8 July, I Corps began its all-out offensive with three divisions - 3rd Canadian, 3rd British and 59th (Staffordshire), supported by two armoured brigades. The Canadians were on the right and by dusk their tanks were on the western outskirts of the city, the 3rd British was into the north east corner, and the 59th was closing in from the north.

The following morning the 3rd Canadian and 3rd British met in the dock area, although the town was not completely cleared for some days.

A Royal Army Service Corps driver recalls:

'After the bombing and fall of Caen we were stationed for a little while in what had been a small German Army hutted camp, the huts made of chipboard - the first time I'd seen this sort of material.

In Caen itself all was devastated. There really was a smell of death in the air, but here and there were pockets where buildings had survived: I remember a particular pen shop stocked with Mont Blanc fountain pens. But most of all, I remember the Cathedral where the "padre" had set up an "English Church". A notice on the door proclaimed:

"We want this to be used as a power house where the spirit can be revived and refreshed to face the struggles of life."

I copied it in my prayer book but this was destroyed when a mortar bomb fell on our kit and I can't be sure if the quote is correct!'

The object of Operation GOODWOOD was to gain the high ground on either side of the Caen-Falaise road and to establish three armoured divisions, the 7th, 11th and Guards, at intervals of nine or ten miles. In the early hours of 18 July the attack started with an artillery barrage coupled with the effect of over 2,999 bombers of the Allied Air Forces. The result was five miles of complete devastation and yet, as the 11th Armoured Division historian tells us, 'beyond and beside these fated acres the enemy waited beside his guns.'

Around the village of Bourguébus, some five miles south of

Caen and to the east of the Falaise road, the 11th Armoured ran into particularly ferocious anti-tank artillery fire and here this Division alone lost over 100 tanks in the first day of the operation.

The result was a static situation and by the third day, when the heavens opened and the scarred land turned into a sea of mud, the scene was akin to a Flanders field of a quarter of a century before.

What GOODWOOD did achieve was the clearing of German pockets of resistance from Caen's eastern and southern suburbs and the strengthening of the Orne Bridgehead, objectives that had been planned for the first day of the invasion and which were vital for the subsequent thrust through France.

Operation COBRA was to start on 25 July near Hebecrevon, west of St Lô, initially with a heavy attack by bombers supported by ground artillery. The bombardment was followed by the American VII Corps attacking with three infantry divisions. Once the flanks had been secured, two armoured divisions and a motorised infantry division were to pass through, driving west and south-east.

The bombardment began at 0940 hours and unfortunately some shells fell on the American lines, killing about 600 of the troops waiting to go into action.

The US Infantry advanced at 1100 hours and at their first objective, Hebecrevon, they met with strong opposition. It was midnight before they achieved success. In other areas resistance was quickly overcome.

The armoured formations advanced as planned and by the 31 July the troops of the German Seventh Army had been driven back along a front: Villedien, Percy, Tessy and le Bény Bocage.

Operation TOTALIZE and the subsequent battle in the Falaise Pocket was probably the most decisive action in Normandy after D-Day. Considerable forces of German armour were attacking the westerly columns of Americans after their breakout in Operation COBRA.

The attack began on 7 August, with General Simmond's II Canadian Corps, reinforced by the British 51st (Highland) Division, 33rd Armoured Brigade and the 1st Polish Armoured Division - newly arrived in France.

An innovation introduced by this operation was the use of improvised armoured troop-carriers called the 'Unfrocked Priests' or 'Holy Rollers' - originally, they had been self-propelled field guns known as Priests and were used on D-Day. Subsequently, they had been replaced by British 25-pounders. With their guns removed they made ideal troop-carriers.

The plan for battle was for the 51st Division and 33rd Armoured Brigade to open the attack to the east of the Falaise road, and 2nd Canadian Division and 2nd Canadian Armoured Brigade to attack the west. Later the 1st Polish and 4th Canadian Armoured Divisions were to pass through to attack the Potigny and Falaise areas.

The target area for the operation, from La Hogue to the Orne was occupied by I SS Panzer Corps and the 89th Infantry Division, behind which was the 12th SS Panzer Division. Also in the area were III Flak Corps and the 272nd Division.

2300 hours 7 August was the moment for the start of a thousand-bomber raid by Bomber Command. Half an hour later the infantry and tanks advanced towards the bombs. As the columns progressed, so a barrage of 360 guns was opened up in front of them, lifted 200 yards every two minutes to allow the assault to continue.

By daybreak several villages had been captured. But the Germans fought back fiercely and much of the success must be attributed to the air attacks made by Typhoons, Spitfires and

Mustangs of the Second Tactical Air Force.

The Battle of Normandy ended on 29 August 1944. Before the war in Europe ended in May 1945 there were other battles, both victories and defeats, to come: Arnhem, The Scheldt Estuary, The Ardennes, the hard winter and then the Rhine Crossing, itself a remarkable amphibious operation. There followed the final tiring weeks of driving into the heart of Germany before the lights of Europe were turned on again.

6 THE COST

It has been said that only some fifty French civilians died in Allied air raids in the April-May run-up to D-Day. This may or may not be true, but in June 1944 bombing from the air and shelling from the bombarding forces caused terrible destruction, particularly in and around Caen and St Lô. Many villages were completely obliterated and heavy fighting during the Allied breakout from the beach-head left numerous areas in ruin and the population in a state of shock.

Caen had seventy-five per cent of its buildings demolished and the country over which land battles were fought became wasteland.

Casualties among French civilians are difficult to estimate but the result of a detailed study of the subject is expected. Early estimates point to between 7,000 and 8,000 victims in Calvados alone. However, all estimates of civilian casualties are complicated by the incalcuable number of people who left Normandy, either voluntarily or by being impressed into forced labour in Germany.

What did strike many Allied servicemen was the way many of the French population in rural areas carried on their day-to-day lives with battle raging around them, ploughing and tending their livestock in close proximity to the combatant forces.

There is no doubt that the French population suffered badly during Operation OVERLORD but, like all civilians throughout the history of warfare, many recovered and even forgave the terrible intrusion of their land and property.

Personal loss, of course, can never be forgotten and there are those who look back to June 1944 as a time of great distress. Allied and German servicemen alike will always feel sadness for what happened to civilians. However, soldiers are under orders and perfoming an unpleasant job; inevitably the innocent are killed or hurt and their property destroyed.

For the armed forces, estimated casualty figures vary greatly. The numbers below are based on the British Official History in which the periods covered depend on nationalities and which service is under review. The figures do not include those for pre-D-Day air operations.

LAND FORCES CASUALTIES 6 JUNE - 31 JUNE 1944

British and Canadian Armies: 3,356 killed, 15,815 wounded and 5,527 missing.
US Army: 5,113 killed, 26,538 wounded and 5,383 missing.
German casualties from 6 June to 7 July have been estimated at 80,783, half of whom were taken prisoners-of-war.

AIR FORCES CASUALTIES 6 JUNE - 31 AUGUST 1944

RAF 2nd Tactical Air Force and Air Defence GB: 1,036 killed or missing, 829 aircraft lost.
RAF Bomber Command: 6,761 killed or missing, 983 aircraft lost.
RAF Coastal Command: 382 killed or missing, 224 aircraft lost.
US 8th Air Force: 7,167 killed or missing, 1,168 aircraft lost.
US 9th Air Force: 1,369 killed or missing, 897 aircraft lost.

APPENDICES

I	AREA AND BEACH CODE NAMES	*47*
II	OPERATIONAL CODE WORDS	*49*
III	COMMAND OF THE ALLIED EXPEDITIONARY FORCE	*54*
IV	ALLIED LAND FORCES	*57*
V	OPERATION NEPTUNE	*79*
VI	ALLIED AIR FORCES	*99*
VII	THE RESISTANCE	*121*
VIII	GERMAN COMMAND IN THE WEST	*124*
IX	GERMAN WEHRMACHT FORCES	*127*
X	GERMAN KRIEGSMARINE FORCES	*135*
XI	THE LUFTWAFFE IN FRANCE	*139*

I AREA AND BEACH CODE NAMES

GOLD — From the eastern extremity of OMAHA beach to the river Provence. The area was divided into three parts: ITEM, JIG and KING beaches.

JUNO — From the eastern extremity of GOLD beach to St Aubin-sur-Mer. The area was divided into three parts: LOVE, MIKE and NAN beaches.

OMAHA — From the river Carentan estuary to the Western extremity of GOLD beach. The area was divided into five parts: CHARLIE, DOG, EASY, FOX, and GEORGE.

SWORD — From the eastern extremity of JUNO to the river Orne. The area was divided into four parts: OBOE, PETER, QUEEN and ROGER. An area to the east of SWORD was code-named BAND, but this beach was not used in the invasion.

UTAH — Northwards from the mouth of the river Vire. The area was divided into two parts: TARE and UNCLE.

II OPERATIONAL CODE WORDS

ANVIL   First name for Allied landings in South of France. Renamed DRAGOON.

ARCADIA   British/US Military Staff Conference, Washington, December 1941 - January 1942.

BENEFICIARY   Plan for breaking out of Normandy assisted by amphibious and airborne assault on St Malo.

BIGOT   Access codeword to top-secret planning for OVERLORD. Used at inter-headquarters communication in England, for documents connected with OVERLORD with a super-classification above 'Top Secret.' Those with clearance to receive BIGOT material were said to be 'bigoted.'

BODYGUARD   Overall deception plan covering Allied strategy in Europe. Plan evolved by two naval, one RAF and five army officers of London Controlling Section (LCS) working in Churchill's underground headquarters in The Mall. Components of overall plan were codenamed FORTITUDE, IRONSIDE, VENDETTA and ZEPPELIN.

BOLERO   US build-up of forces and equipment for OVERLORD.

BOMBARDON   Floating steel breakwaters for MULBERRY harbours.

BULBASKET   Special Air Service operation of 5-6 June to

	block the Paris-Bordeaux railway near Poitiers.
COBRA	US First Army operation to break out of Normandy bridgehead. Operation launched 25th July 1944.
CONEBO	RAF Coastal Command operations against light German naval forces.
CORE	Patrol operations aimed at preventing German U Boats from entering English Channel from the west.
CORNCOB	Blockships forming part of GOOSEBERRY breakwaters.
CROSSBOW	Preventative Allied measures against V1 and V2 weapons.
DRAGOON	See ANVIL.
EPSOM	British Second Army offensive near Caen, July 1944.
EUREKA	Teheran Conference, November - December 1943.
FABIUS	Allied amphibious exercises, May 1944.
FORTITUDE	Deception plan covering OVERLORD. FORTITUDE SOUTH aimed to convince the enemy that there would be a massive invasion in the Pas de Calais area. The operation used a fictitious US Army Group codenamed QUICKSILVER. Dummy camps, tanks, aircraft and landing craft supported the allusion, and bogus radio traffic (codenamed ROSEBUD) was

provided by wireless trucks moving around the south-east of England. A lesser operation, FORTITUDE NORTH was meant to create the impression that Allied landings would be made in Norway.

GAIN	Special Air Service operation of 5-6 June to lay night-time road ambushes southwest of Paris.
GOODWOOD	British breakout attack coinciding with US Operation COBRA, July 1944.
GOOSEBERRY	Artificial breakwaters for MULBERRY harbours and offshore anchorages.
HANDS-UP	Plan for breaking out of Normandy assisted by amphibious and airbourne assault on Quiberon Bay, Brittany.
HORNPIPE	Code word covering message to Allied forces advising 24 hour delay of invasion because of bad weather.
HOUNSWORTH	Special Air Service operation of 5-6 June in the Forêt du Morvan to disrupt German troop movements in northern Burgundy.
IRONSIDE	A deception operation designed to keep a German Army in the Bordeaux area for at least three weeks after D-Day.
MAPLE	Mine-laying part of NEPTUNE.
MASTER	US First Army signals code word.
MULBERRY	Artificial harbours.
NEPTUNE	Naval operational part of OVERLORD.

PHOENIX	Concrete caissons used as breakwaters for MULBERRY harbours.
PIRATE	British and Canadian (Task Force J) exercise.
PLUTO	Pipe Line Under The Ocean for supplying petrol from England to the Continent.
POINTBLANK	Allied bomber offensive against Germany.
QUADRANT	First Quebec Conference, August 1943.
RANKIN	Contingency plan for use in the event of German surrender prior to OVERLORD.
RATTLE	Combined Operations conference on amphibious tactics.
ROB ROY	Drop of resupplies of food, ammunition, explosives, medical stores, petrol and equipment; carried out by 38 and 46 Groups RAF.
SEXTANT	Cairo Conference December 1943.
SHARPENER	SHAEF Advance HQ at Portsmouth, May 1944. Later enlarged and renamed SHIP MATE.
SHELLBURST	SHAEF Advance HQ in Normandy, June 1944.
SHIPMATE	See SHARPENER.
SPRING	Canadian Army attack in Normandy, coinciding with US Operation COBRA and British Operation GOODWOOD, July 1944.

SWAMP	RAF Coastal Command operations covering attack on German U Boats in support of OVERLORD.
SWORDHILT	Plan for amphibious and airborne seizure of area east of Brest.
SYMBOL	Casablanca Conference, January 1943.
TIGER	US VII Corps (Force U) invasion exercise.
TOMBOLA	Pipeline supply of petrol from tankers for storage in Normandy.
TOPFLIGHT	Release of press information on OVERLORD landings.
TRIDENT	Washington Conference, May 1943.
VENDETTA	Deception Operation aimed to keep the maximum number of German troops in the South of France. The actual invasion of the South of France was code-named ANVIL.
WHALE	Floating steel pierheads for MULBERRY harbours and roadways to shore.
WIDEWING	SHAEF headquarters at Bushy Park near London.
ZEBRA	US Air Force mass drop of supplies to French Resistance (Maquis), 25th June 1944.
ZEPPELIN	Deception threat of invasion of Balkans and southern France to mask OVERLORD.

III COMMAND OF THE ALLIED EXPEDITIONARY FORCE

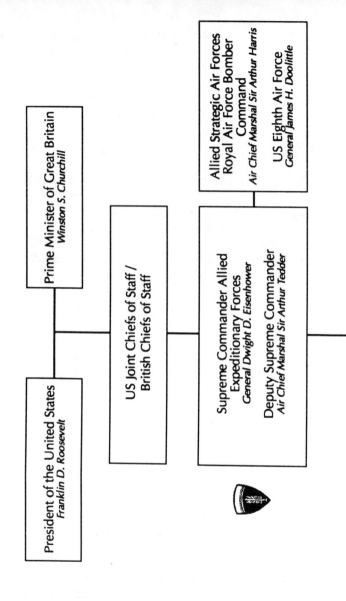

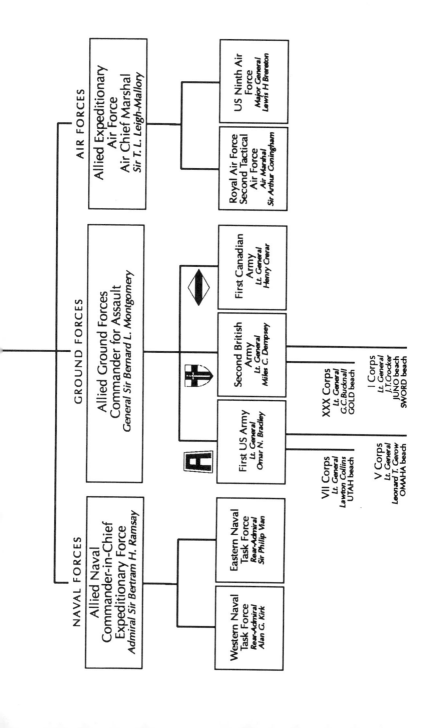

IV ALLIED LAND FORCES

AREA: UTAH. VII CORPS OF US FIRST ARMY

AIRBORNE DIVISIONS ATTACHED TO VII CORPS FOR OPERATION OVERLORD

82nd AIRBORNE DIVISION
(Major General Matthew Ridgeway)

505th Parachute Infantry Regiment
507th Parachute Infantry Regiment
506th Parachute Infantry Regiment
325th Glider Infantry Regiment
456th Parachute Field Artillery Battalion
319th Glider Field Artillery Battalion
320th Glider Field Artillery Battalion
80th Glider Anti-Aircraft Artillery Battalion - in anti-tank role
307th Airborne Engineer Battalion
307th Airborne Medical Company
782nd Airborne Ordnance Maintenance Company
407th Airborne Quartermaster Company
82nd Airborne Signal Company
82nd Airborne Military Police Platoon
82nd Airborne Reconnaissance Company

101st AIRBORNE DIVISION
(Major General Maxwell D. Taylor)

501st Parachute Infantry Regiment
502nd Parachute Infantry Regiment
506th Parachute Infantry Regiment
327th Glider Infantry Regiment (initial follow-up formation)
401st (part of) Glider Infantry Regiment
377th Parachute Field Artillery Battalion
321st Glider Field Artillery Battalion
907th Glider Field Artillery Battalion

81st Airborne Anti-Aircraft Battalion - in anti-tank role
326th Airborne Engineer Battalion
326th Airborne Medical Company
801st Airborne Ordnance Maintenance Company
426th AIrborne Quartermaster Company
101st Airborne Signal Company
101st Airborne Military Police Platoon
101st Airborne Reconnaissance Company

US SEABORNE FORCES: VII CORPS

St MARCOUF FORCE attached to VII for Operation OVERLORD

4th US Cavalry Squadron
24th US Cavalry Squadron
This force landed at 0430 hours on St Marcouf Islands about four miles off the mainland. The landing was unopposed.

4 DIVISION GROUP (UTAH BEACH LANDING FORCE)

4th INFANTRY DIVISION
(Major General Raymond O. Barton)

8th Infantry Regiment
12th Infantry Regiment
22nd Infantry Regiment
20th Field Artillery Battalion
29th Field Artillery Battalion
42nd Field Artillery Battalion
44th Field Artillery Battalion
Divisional Artillery was augmented by guns from the:
90th Infantry Division
4th Reconnaissance Troop
70th Tank Battalion from 6th Armoured Group - with Duplex-Drive tanks
4th Engineer Combat Battalion, augmented by Clearance

Teams from 1st Engineer Special Brigade
4th Medical Battalion
704th Ordnance Light Maintenance Company
4th Quartermaster Company
4th Signal Company
4th Military Police Platoon

FOLLOW-UP DIVISIONS OF VII CORPS

90TH INFANTRY DIVISION
(Major General Jay W. MacKelvie), landed D-Day - D+14

357th Infantry Regiment
358th Infantry Regiment
359th Infantry Regiment
Usual Divisional Troops

9th INFANTRY DIVISION
(Major General Manton S. Eddy), landed D+4

39th Infantry Regiment
47th Infantry Regiment
60th Infantry Regiment
Usual Divisional Troops

79TH INFANTRY DIVISION
(Major General Ira T. Wyche), landed D+4 - D+8

313rd Infantry Regiment
314th Infantry Regiment
315th Infantry Regiment
Usual Divisional Troops

AREA: OMAHA. V CORPS OF US FIRST ARMY

✝ DIVISION GROUP (OMAHA BEACH LANDING FORCE)

1st INFANTRY DIVISION
(Major General Clarence R. Huebner)

16th REGIMENTAL COMBAT TEAM
16th Infantry Regiment
7th Field Artillery Battalion
1st and 20th Engineer Combat Battalions
1st (A Company) Medical Battalion
741st Tank Battalion with Duplex-Drive tanks from 3rd Armoured Group
62nd Armoured Field Artillery Battalion

18th REGIMENTAL COMBAT TEAM
18th Infantry Regiment
5th and 32nd Field Artillery Battalions
1st (B Company) Engineer Combat Battalion
1st (B and D Companies) Medical Battalion
745th Tank Battalion

26th REGIMENTAL COMBAT TEAM
26th Infantry Regiment
33rd Field Artillery Battalion
1st (C Company) Engineer Combat Battalion
1st (C Company) Medical Battalion
Plus usual Divisional Troops: Ordnance Maintenance, Quartermaster, Signals, Military Police and Reconnaissance units

Also under 1st Infantry Division Command:
5th and 6th Special Engineer Brigades
81st Chemical Battalion

PROVISIONAL RANGER GROUP
(Lieutenant Colonel James E. Rudder)

2nd Ranger Battalion
5th Ranger Battalion

FOLLOW-UP DIVISIONS OF V CORPS

29th INFANTRY DIVISION
(Major General Charles H. Gerhardt) landed D+1

115th Infantry Regiment (known as 1st Maryland)
116th Infantry Regiment (known as The Stonewall Brigade)
175th Infantry Regiment (known as 5th Maryland
110th Field Artillery Battalion
111th Field Artillery Battalion
224th Field Artillery Battalion
227th Field Attillery Battalion
121st Engineer Battalion
104th Medical Battalion
729th Ordnance Company
Plus usual Divisional Troops: Quartermaster, Signals, Military Police and Reconnaissance units

2nd INFANTRY DIVISION
(Major General Walter M. Robertson) landed D+1

9th Infantry Regiment
23rd Infantry Regiment
38th Infantry Regiment
12th Field Artillery Battalion
15th Field Artillery Battalion
37th Field Artillery Battalion
38th Field Artillery Battalion
2nd Engineer Combat Battalion
2nd Medical Battalion
2nd Signal Company
2nd Reconnaissance Troops

Plus usual Divisional Troops: Ordnance, Quartermaster and Military Police units.

Also under 2nd Infantry Division command:
612th Tank Destroyer Battalion
635th Tank Destroyer Battalion
741st Tank Battalion
747th Tank Battalion

2nd ARMORED DIVISION
(Major General Edward H. Brooks) landed D+1 - D+3

COMBAT COMMAND A
66th Armor
41st Armored Infantry
14th Armored Field Artillery Battalion
17th (A Company) Armored Engineer Battalion
48th (A Company) Armored Medical Battalion
2nd (A Company) Armored Ordnance Maintenance Battalion
2nd (A Company) Armored Division Supply Battalion

COMBAT COMMAND B
67th Armor
41st (1st Battalion) Armored Infantry
78th Armored Field Artillery Battalion
17th (B Company) Armored Engineer Battalion
48th (B Company) Armored Medical Battalion
2nd (B Company) Armored Ordnance Maintenance Battalion
2nd (B Company) Armored Division Supply Battalion

RESERVE AND DIVISIONAL TROOPS
195th Anti-Aircraft Artillery Automatic Weapons Battalion
95th Armoured Field Artillery Battalion
702nd Tank Destroyer Battalion
82nd Reconnaissance Battalion
142nd Armored Signal Company
165th (F Detachment) Signal Photo Company
Military Police Platoon
608th (1st Platoon) Quartermaster Company

AREAS: GOLD, JUNO AND SWORD. I CORPS AND XXX CORPS OF BRITISH SECOND ARMY

79th ARMOURED DIVISION
(Major General Sir Percy C. S. Hobart)

Detachments of specialised armour from this Division supported landings on all three British and Canadian beaches.

30th ARMOURED BRIGADE (Flail tanks)
22nd Dragoons
1st Lothian and Border Horse
2nd County of London Yeomanry (Westminster Dragoons)
141st Regiment, Royal Armoured Corps

1st TANK BRIGADE
11th Battalion Royal Tank Regiment
42nd Battalion Royal Tank Regiment
49th Battalion Royal Tank Regiment

1st ASSAULT BRIGADE, ROYAL ENGINEERS (AVREs and Buffaloes)
5th Assault Regiment RE
6th Assault Regiment RE
42nd Assault Regiment RE

DIVISIONAL TROOPS
79th Armoured Divisional Signals
1st Canadian Armoured Personnel Carrier Regiment (Crocodiles)

AREA: GOLD. XXX CORPS OF BRITISH SECOND ARMY

50 DIVISION GROUP (GOLD BEACH LANDING FORCE)

50th (NORTHUMBRIAN) DIVISION
(Major General D. A. H. Graham)

69th BRIGADE (assault brigade)
5th Battalion The East Yorkshire Regiment
6th Battalion The Green Howards
7th Battalion The Green Howards

151st BRIGADE
6th Battalion The Durham Light Infantry
8th Battalion The Durham Light Infantry
9th Battalion The Durham Light Infantry

231st BRIGADE (assault brigade)
2nd Battalion The Devonshire Regiment
1st Battalion The Hampshire Regiment
1st Battalion The Dorsetshire Regiment

DIVISIONAL TROOPS
61st Reconnaissance Regiment RAC
86th, 90th and 147th Field Regiments RA detached from Corps Troops (self-propelled guns)
74th and 124th Field Regiments RA
102nd Anti-Tank Regiment RA
25 th Light Anti-Aircraft Regiment RA
50th Divisional Engineers
50th Divisional Signals
2nd Battalion The Cheshire Regiment (machine-gun)
Plus usual Medical, Ordnance, Service and Military Police Divisional units.

47 ROYAL MARINE COMMANDO OF 4 SPECIAL SERVICE BRIGADE
(Lieutenant-Colonel C. F. Phillips)

Landed with 231st Brigade at Gold beach with Port-en-Bessin as objective

1 ROYAL MARINE ARMOURED SUPPORT REGIMENT

56th INDEPENDENT INFANTRY BRIGADE
2nd Battalion The South Wales Borderers
2nd Battalion The Gloucestershire Regiment
2nd Battalion The Essex Regiment

8th ARMOURED BRIGADE
4th/7th Dragoon Guards
24th Lancers
The Nottinghamshire Yeomanry
12th Battalion The King's Royal Rifle Corps (Motor)

FOLLOW-UP FORCES ON GOLD BEACH

7th ARMOURED DIVISION
(Major General G. W. E. J. Erskine) landed D+2

22nd ARMOURED BRIGADE
1st Battalion The Royal Tank Regiment
5th Battalion The Royal Tank Regiment
4th Battalion The County of London Yeomanry
5th Battalion The Royal Inniskilling Dragoon Guards

131st (QUEEN'S) BRIGADE
1/5th, 1/6th, 1/7th Battalions The Queen's Royal Regiment
No 3 Support Company The Royal Northumberland Fusiliers

DIVISIONAL TROOPS
8th Hussars
11th Hussars
3rd Battalion The Royal Horse Artillery
5th Battalions The Royal Horse Artillery
15th Light Anti-Aircraft Regiment RA
65th Anti-Tank Regiment RA
4th Field Squadron RE
621st Field Squadron RE
143rd Field Park Squadron RE
7th Armoured Divisional Signals
Plus usual Divisional units

49th (WEST RIDING) DIVISION
(Major General Evelyn Barker) landed D+6

70th BRIGADE
10th Battalion The Durham Light Infantry
11th Battalion The Durham Light Infantry
1st Battalion The Tyneside Scottish

146th BRIGADE
4th Battalion The Lincolnshire Regiment
1/4th Battalion The King's Own Yorkshire Light Infantry
The Hallamshire Battalion The York & Lancashire Regiment

147th BRIGADE
11th Battalion The Royal Scots Fusiliers
6th Battalion The Duke of Wellington's Regiment

7th Battalion The Duke of Wellington's Regiment

DIVISIONAL TROOPS
49th Reconnaissance Regiment RAC
69th Field Regiment RA
143rd Field Regiment RA
185th Field Regiment RA
55th Anti-Tank Regiment (The Suffolk Yeomanry) RA
89th Light Anti-Aircraft Regiment RA
49th Divisional Engineers
49th Divisional Signals
2nd Battalion The Princess Louise's Kensington Regiment (machine-gun)
Plus usual Divisional Medical, Ordnance, Service and Military Police units.

33rd ARMOURED BRIGADE
1st Battalion The Northamptonshire Yeomanary
144th Regiment RAC
148th Regiment RAC

AREA: JUNO. I CORPS OF BRITISH SECOND ARMY

3 CANADIAN DIVISION GROUP (JUNO BEACH LANDING AREA)

3rd CANADIAN DIVISION
(Major-General R. F. L. Keller)

7th CANADIAN BRIGADE (assault brigade)
The Royal Winnipeg Rifles
The Regina Rifle Regiment
1st Battalion The Canadian Scottish Rifles

8th CANADIAN BRIGADE (assault brigade)
The Queen's Own Rifles of Canada
Le Régiment de la Chandière
The North Shore (New Brunswick) Regiment

9th CANADIAN BRIGADE
The Highland Light Infantry of Canada
The Stormont, Dundas and Glengarry Highlanders
The North Nova Scotia Highlanders

DIVISIONAL TROOPS
7th Reconnaissance Regiment (17th Duke of York's Royal Canadian Hussars)
19th Field Regiment RCA (self-propelled guns with assault brigades)
12th, 13th and 14th Field Regiments RCA
3rd Anti-Tank Regiment RCA
4th Light Anti-Aircraft Regiment RCA
3rd Canadian Divisional Engineers
3rd Canadian Divisional Signals
The Cameron Highlanders of Ottawa (machine-gun)
Plus usual Medical, Ordnance, Service and Military Police Divisional units.

2nd CANADIAN ARMOURED BRIGADE
(Duplex-Drive tanks)

6th Armoured Regiment (1st Hussars)
10th Armoured Regiment (The Fort Garry Horse)
27th Armoured Regiment (The Sherbrooke Fusiliers Regiment)

4 SPECIAL SERVICE BRIGADE HEADQUARTERS
(Brigadier B. W. Leicester)

48 Royal Marine Commando (Lieutenant Colonel J. L. Moulton)
Other units of 4 Special Service Brigade landed on GOLD and SWORD beaches.

2 ROYAL MARINE ARMOURED SUPPORT REGIMENT

FOLLOW-UP FORMATIONS ON JUNO BEACH

51st (HIGHLAND) DIVISION
(Major General D. C. Bullen-Smith) landed D+1

152nd BRIGADE
2nd Battalion The Seaforth Highlanders
5th Battalion The Seaforth Highlanders
5th Battalion The Queen's Own Cameron Highlanders

153rd BRIGADE
5th Battalion The Black Watch
1st Battalion The Gordon Highlanders
5th/7th Battalion The Gordon Highlanders

154th BRIGADE
1st Battalion The Black Watch
7th Battalion The Black Watch
7th Battalion The Argyll & Sutherland Highlanders

DIVISIONAL TROOPS
2nd Derbyshire Yeomanry RAC
126th Field Regiment RA
127th Field Regiment RA
128th Field Regiment RA
61st Anti-Tank Regiment RA
40th Light Anti-Aircraft Regiment RA
51st Divisional Engineers
51st Divisional Signals
1/7th Battalion The Middlesex Regiment (machine-gun)
Plus usual Divisional Medical, Ordnance, Service and Military Police units.

4th INDEPENDENT ARMOURED BRIGADE

The Royal Scots Greys
3rd County of London Yeomanry (Sharpshooters)
44th Battalion The Royal Tank Regiment
2nd Battalion The King's Royal Rifle Corps

AREA: SWORD. I CORPS OF BRITISH SECOND ARMY

AIRBORNE DIVISION UNDER I CORPS COMMAND AFTER LANDING

6th AIRBORNE DIVISION
(Major-General R. N. Gale)

3rd PARACHUTE BRIGADE
8th Battalion The Parachute Regiment
1st Canadian Battalion The Parachute Regiment
9th Battalion The Parachute Regiment

5th PARACHUTE BRIGADE
7th Battalion The Parachute Regiment
12th Battalion The Parachute Regiment
13th Battalion The Parachute Regiment

6th AIRLANDING BRIGADE
12th Battalion The Devonshire Regiment
2nd Battalion The Oxfordshire and Buckinghamshire Light Infantry
1st Battalion The Royal Ulster Rifles

DIVISIONAL TROOPS
6th Airborne Armoured Reconnaissance Regiment RAC
53rd Airlanding Light Regiment RA
6th Airborne Engineers
6th Airborne Signals
Plus usual Divisional Medical, Ordnance, Service and Military Police units.

ATTACHED TO 6th AIRBORNE DIVISION
1st Glider Pilot Wing The Glider Pilot Regiment
2nd Glider Pilot Wing The Glider Pilot Regiment

SEABORNE FORCES

3 DIVISION GROUP (SWORD BEACH LANDING FORCE)

3rd DIVISION
(Major-General T. G. Rennie)

8th BRIGADE (assault brigade)
1st Battalion The Suffolk Regiment
2nd Battalion The East Yorkshire Regiment
1st Battalion The South Lancashire Regiment

9th BRIGADE
2nd Battalion The Lincolnshire Regiment
1st Battalion The King's Own Scottish Borderers
2nd Battalion The Royal Ulster Rifles

185th BRIGADE
2nd Battalion The Royal Warwickshire Regiment
1st Battalion The Royal Norfolk Regiment
2nd Battalion The King's Own Shropshire Light Infantry

DIVISIONAL TROOPS
3rd Reconnaissance Regiment RAC
33rd and 76th Field Regiments RA (self-propelled guns)
7th Field Regiment RA
20th Anti-Tank Regiment RA
92nd Light Anti-Aircraft Regiment RA
3rd Divisional Engineers
3rd Divisional Signals
2nd Battalion The Middlesex Regiment (machine-gun)
Plus usual Medical, Ordnance, Service and M P Div. units.

5 ROYAL MARINE ARMOURED SUPPORT
REGIMENT

27th INDEPENDENT ARMOURED BRIGADE
(D-D tanks)

13th/18th Royal Hussars
1st East Riding Yeomanry
The Staffordshire Yeomanry

SPECIAL SERVICE BRIGADE GROUP
(Major-General G. Sturges RM)

1 SPECIAL SERVICE BRIGADE - landed on eastern extremity of SWORD
(Brigadier Lord Lovat)

3 Commando (Lieutenant Colonel Peter Young)
4 Commando (Lieutenant Colonel Robert Dawson)
6 Commando (Lieutenant Colonel Derek Mills-Roberts)
45 Royal Marine Commando (Lieutenant Colonel Charles Ries)
A force of 176 French Marine Commandos from 10 (Inter-Allied) Commando led by Commandant Phillippe de Vaisseau Kieffer landed on SWORD beach with 4 Commando.

4 SPECIAL SERVICE BRIGADE - landed between JUNO and SWORD

41 Royal Marine Commando - landed Lion-sur-Mer (Lieutenant Colonel T. M. Gray)
46 Royal Marine Commando - landed D+1 in support of Canadian 3rd Division (Lieutenant Colonel Campbell Hardy)
47 Royal Marine Commando - landed GOLD. Objective Port-en-Bessin (Lieutenant Colonel C. F. Phillips)
48 Royal Marine Commando - landed JUNO. Fought towards St Aubin-sur-Mer (Lieutenant Colonel J. L. Moulton)
Brigade HQ landed on eastern extremity of JUNO beach with 47 Royal Marine Commando.

ALSO ENGAGED DURING THE OVERLORD ASSAULT

1st and 2nd Special Air Service Regiments, including Free French Parachute Battalions.

ALLIED ARMY ORGANISATION

An ARMY GROUP in the Second World War was composed of two or more ARMIES. In the case of the 21st Army Group at the time of D-Day these were British Second Army and US First Army (hence the designation '21st' Army Group). In addition, an Army Group had in its establishment its own GHQ Troops, Lines of Communication Troops and Base Installations.

An Army was composed of two or more CORPS and Army Troops. A Corps consisted of two or more DIVISIONS plus Corps Troops.

A Corps could also have on its strength INDEPENDENT BRIGADES which had either Infantry, Armoured or Special Service (Commando) roles.

The organisation was flexible in that the Corps could be transferred from one Army to another. Similarly, Divisions were often transferred from one Corps to another during a campaign.

British front line Divisions were of three types: Armoured, Infantry and Airborne. An Armoured Division was composed of one Armoured Brigade (3 Regiments and 1 Motor Battalion) and one Infantry Brigade (3 Battalions).

An Infantry Division had three Infantry Brigades (total of 9 Battalions).

An Airborne Division consisted of two Parachute Brigades and one Airlanding (Glider) Brigade (total of 9 Battalions).

In addition, all Divisions had their complement of Reconnaissance, Artillery, Engineers, Signals, Machine Gun, Supply and Transport, Medical, Ordnance, Workshop and Provost Units.

Manpower strength was 15,000 for Armoured, 18,000 for Infantry and 12,000 for Airborne Divisions.

The Independent Armoured Brigades were composed of three Regiments of Battalions with a total manpower strength of about 3,000 of all ranks.

There were some important differences between British and American military formation organisation.

The US Infantry Division consisted of three Infantry Regiments (9 Battalions), each Regiment including two companies of Artillery (1 of howitzers and 1 anti-tank). Each Battalion had its Rifle Companies and one Heavy Weapons Company equipped with mortars and machine guns. In the Infantry Division, there were also four Battalions of Field Artillery with a total of 48 guns.

Generally, US Armored Divisions comprised three Battalions of tanks and three Battalions of Infantry which operated in two Combat Commands. The number of tanks was about 270 and in addition there were 36 self-propelled howitzers. Manpower strength was about 14,000 for Infantry, 11,000 for Armored and 9,000 for Airborne Divisions.

SPECIALISED TRACKED VEHICLES

DUPLEX DRIVE TANK - Some nine hundred M4 Sherman tanks were made amphibious for the D-Day landings by fitting a collapsible flotation screen round the hull. The tanks were also equipped with propellers for use when in the sea - hence the designation 'Duplex Drive', usually abbreviated to 'DD'.

The British 79th Armoured Division, commanded by Major-General Sir Percy Hobart, was affectionately known as 'The Zoo'. The Division's establishment consisted of specially developed or adapted tracked vehicles. These 'Hobart's Funnies' were available to all formations of the 21st Army Group as required.

The vehicles of the 79th Armoured Division were known by the following names:

ARK or Armoured Ramp Carrier, sometimes known as 'Scissors Bridge' - Folding ramps mounted fore and aft on a Churchill tank hull. In operation the tank was driven into a defensive ditch and the ramps lowered. Other vehicles could then drive over the ramps and tank hull.

AVRE or Armoured Vehicle, Royal Engineers - Churchill tank fitted with a 290 mm mortar or petard in place of a gun for use against pillboxes and other concrete structures. The 40 lbs demolition charge had a range of up to 80 yards. The vehicle was also used as a carrier for assault engineers.

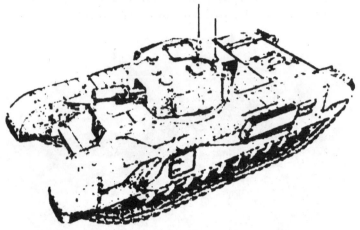

BOBBIN or Track Layer - Tank carrying a roll of metal mesh that could be unrolled to form a trackway over marshy ground.

BRIDGE LAYER - Churchill tank carrying a bridge section to span a short gap. The 4.8 tons section was hydraulically set in place across the gap.

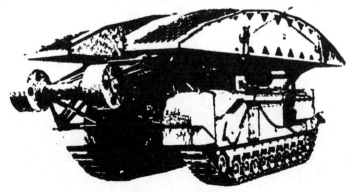

BUFFALO or ALLIGATOR Tracked Landing Vehicle - Not a tank but a specially designed tracked amphibious vehicle capable of carrying personnel or a Jeep.

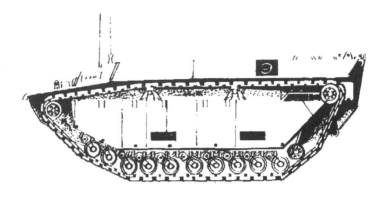

CDL - Tank equipped with a very bright light that could be focussed to blind defensive positions at night.

CONGER - Churchill tank equipped with mine-clearing hose-pipes filled with explosive.

CRAB - Another mine-clearing armoured vehicle. Usually a Sherman fitted with a chain-flail on extended arms at the front. The flails exploded mines and provided a 9 ft wide safe route through which other tanks could follow. Operating speed: about 1.5 mph.

CROCODILE - Flame-thrower tank, usually a Churchill. The fuel for the weapon was carried in a two-wheeled 400 gallon armoured trailer. Range of fire: about 80 yards.

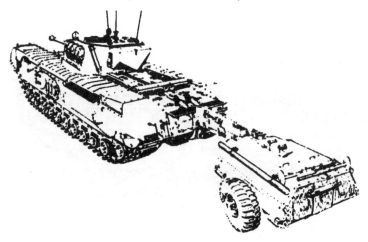

FASCINE CARRIER - Tank with an 8 ft diameter bundle of chestnut paling mounted at the front which could be released to fill a crater or ditch.

KANGAROO - Tank with turret removed and used for conveying troops. Before the Battle of Falaise a number of Priest Self-Propelled Guns had their armament removed so the vehicles could be used for troop-carrying. These were given the semi-official name of DEFROCKED PRIESTS.

TANKDOZER - Tank fitted with a bulldozer blade at the front

V OPERATION NEPTUNE

ALLIED NAVAL COMMAND

Allied Naval Commander-in-Chief Expeditionary Force (ANCXF): Admiral Sir Bertram H. Ramsay RN.
Chief-of-Staff: Rear-Admiral G. E. Creasy RN.
Chief Naval Administrative Officer and Flag Officer British Assault Area: Rear-Admiral J. W. Rivett-Carnac RN.
Flag Officer West: Rear-Admiral J. Wilkes USN.
Rear-Admiral Mulberry/Pluto (Pre-fabricated harbours and Pipe Line under the Ocean): Rear-Admiral W.G. Tennant RN.

NAVAL FORCES

WESTERN NAVAL TASK FORCE, TF 123 (for US landing beaches): Rear-Admiral A. G. Kirk USN aboard cruiser USS *Augusta*.
EASTERN NAVAL TASK FORCE (for British and Canadian landing beaches): Rear-Admiral Sir Philip Vian RN aboard HMS *Scylla*.
BOMBARDING FORCE A (Utah beach area): Rear-Admiral M. L. Deyo USN aboard cruiser USS *Tuscaloosa*.
BOMBARDING FORCE C (Omaha beach area): Rear-Admiral C. F. Bryant USN aboard battleship USS *Texas*.
BOMBARDING FORCE K (Gold beach area): Captain E. W. L. Longley-Cook RN aboard cruiser HMS *Argonaut*.
BOMBARDING FORCE E (Juno beach area): Rear-Admiral F. H. G. Dalrymple-Hamilton RN aboard cruiser HMS *Belfast* (now preserved as a museum in London).
BOMBARDING FORCE D (Sword and Band beaches areas): Rear-Admiral W. R. Patterson RN aboard cruiser HMS *Mauritius*.
ASSAULT FORCE U, TF 125 (Utah beach): Rear-Admiral D. P. Moon USN aboard headquarters ship USS *Bayfield*, commanding 12 convoys.

ASSAULT FORCE O, TF 124 (Omaha beach): Rear-Admiral J. L. Hall Jr USN aboard headquarters ship USS *Ancon*, commanding 9 convoys..
ASSAULT FORCE G (Gold beach): Commodore C. E. Douglas-Pennant RN aboard headquarters ship HMS *Bulolo*, commanding 16 convoys.
ASSAULT FORCE J (Juno beach): Commodore G. N. Oliver RN aboard headquarters ship HMS *Hilary*, commanding 10 convoys.
ASSAULT FORCE S (Sword beach): Rear-Admiral A. G. Talbot RN aboard headquarters ship HMS *Largs*, commanding 12 convoys.
FOLLOW-UP FORCE B, TF 126 (for US landing beaches): Commodore C. D. Edgar USN aboard destroyer USS *Maloy*.
FOLLOW-UP FORCE L (For British and Canadian landing beaches): Rear-Admiral W. E. Parry RN with headquarters ashore.
DEPOT SHIPS: Commodore H. T. England RN aboard cruiser HMS *Hawkins*.

NAVAL OFFICERS ASHORE

UTAH BEACH: Captain J. E. Arnold USN.
OMAHA BEACH: Captain Camp USN.
GOLD BEACH: Captain G. V. M. Dolphin RN.
JUNO BEACH: Captain C. D. Maud RN.
*SWORD BEACH:*Captain W. R. C. Leggatt RN.

SHIPS ENGAGED IN NEPTUNE

An astonishing armada of 6,939 vessels of all sizes took part in Operation Neptune, including 1,213 warships. In addition, 736 ancillary ships and craft carried out roles such as buoy-laying, smoke-making and telephone-cable laying, and a further 864 merchant ships were employed in logistic capacities.

The listing below consists of many of the named vessels but does not include ships and craft identified only by number, nor the ancillary and merchant ships which were not directly connected with the assault operations on D-Day.

BATTLESHIPS

USS *Arkansas*	Bombarding Force C
HMS *Nelson*	General Reserve
USS *Nevada*	Bombarding Force A
HMS *Ramillies*	Bombarding Force D
HMS *Rodney*	Eastern Task Force Reserve
USS *Texas*	Flagship Bombarding Force C
HMS *Warspite*	Bombarding Force D

HEADQUARTERS SHIPS

USS *Ancon*	Flagship Assault Force O
USS *Bayfield*	Flagship Assault Force U
HMS *Bulolo*	Flagship Assault Force G
HMS *Hilary*	Flagship Assault Force J
HMS *Largs*	Flagship Assault Force S

CRUISERS

HMS *Ajax*	Bombarding Force K
HMS *Arathusa*	Bombarding Force D
HMS *Argonaut*	Bombarding Force K
USS *Augusta*	Flagship Western Task Force
HMS *Belfast*	Flagship Bombarding Force E
HMS *Bellona*	Western Task Force Reserve
HMS *Black Prince*	Bombarding Force A
HMS *Capetown*	Western Task Force Far Shore Shuttle Control
HMS *Danae*	Bombarding Force D
HMS *Diadem*	Bombarding Force E

ORP *Dragon*	Bombarding Force E - Polish Navy
HMS *Emerald*	Bombarding Force E
HMS *Enterprise*	Bombarding Force A
HMS *Frobisher*	Bombarding Force D
FFS *Georges Leygues*	Bombarding Force C - Free French Navy
HMS *Glasgow*	Bombarding Force C
HMS *Hawkins*	Bombarding Force A
HMS *Mauritius*	Flagship Bombarding Force D
FFS *Montcalm*	Bombarding Force C
HMS *Orion*	Bombarding Force K
USS *Quincy*	Bombarding Force A
HMS *Scylla*	Flagship Eastern Task Force
HMS *Sirius*	Eastern Task Force Reserve
USS *Tuscaloosa*	Flagship Bombarding Force A

DESTROYERS AND DESTROYER ESCORTS

HMS *Albrighton*	Escort vessel Gold beach
HMCS *Algonquin*	Force E - Royal Canadian Navy
USS *Amesbury*	Escort vessel Omaha beach
HMS *Ashanti*	10th Destroyer Flotilla
USS *Baldwin*	Force C
USS *Barton*	Escort vessel Utah beach
HMS *Beagle*	Force J
USS *Bates*	Force U
HMS *Blankney*	Force E
USS *Bleasdale*	Force E
USS *Blessman*	Escort vessel Omaha beach
ORP *Blyscawica*	10th Destroyer Flotilla
USS *Borum*	Escort vessel Omaha beach
HMS *Brissenden*	Escort vessel Western Task Force
USS *Butler*	Force A
HMS *Campbell*	Force S
USS *Carnick*	Force C
HMS *Cattistock*	Force K
USS *Corry*	Force A (sunk)
HMS *Cotswold*	Force L

HMS *Cottesmore*	Force K
USS *Doyle*	Force C
HMS *Eglinton*	Force D
USS *Ellyson*	Western Task Force Omaha beach
USS *Emmons*	Force C
HMS *Eskimo*	10th Destroyer Flotilla
USS *Fitch*	Force A
USS *Forrest*	Force A Western Force Flagship Group
USS *Frankford*	Escort vessel Omaha beach
HMS *Fury*	Force E
USS *Gherardi*	Force U
HNMS *Glaisdale*	Force E - Norwegian Navy
USS *Glennon*	Escort vessel Utah beach (sunk)
HMS *Goathland*	Escort vessel Force S
HMS *Grenville*	Force K
HMCS *Haida*	10th Destroyer Flotilla
USS *Hambleton*	Force B
USS *Harding*	Force C
USS *Herndon*	Force A
USS *Hobson*	Force A
HMCS *Huron*	10th Destroyer Flotilla
HMS *Impulsive*	Force D
HMS *Javelin*	10th Destroyer Flotilla
USS *Jeffers*	Escort vessel Utah beach
HMS *Jervis*	Force K
HMS *Kelvin*	Force D
HMS *Kempenfelt*	Force E
HMS *Keppel*	Escort vessel
ORP *Krakowiak*	Force K
FFS *Combattante*	Force E
USS *Laffey*	Escort vessel Utah beach
HMS *Mackay*	Escort vessel
USS *Maloy*	Escort vessel Western Task Force
USS *McCook*	Force C
HMS *Melbreak*	Force C
USS *Meredith*	Escort vessel Utah beach (sunk)
HMS *Middleton*	Force D
USS *Murphy*	Force O

USS *Nelson*	Escort vessel Omaha beach (sunk)
USS *O'Brien*	Force U
ORP *Piorun*	10th Destroyer Flotilla
USS *Plunkett*	Force O
HMS *Pytchley*	Force K
USS *Rich*	Force U (sunk)
USS *Rodman*	Force B
USS *Satterlee*	Western Task Force
HMS *Saumarez*	Force D
HMS *Scorpion*	Force D
HMS *Scourge*	Force D
HMS *Serapis*	Force D
HMCS *Sioux*	Force E
USS *Shubrick*	Force A
ORP *Slazak*	Force D
HMS *Stevenstone*	Force E
HNMS *Stord*	Force D
HNMS *Svenner*	Force D (sunk by E Boats in action)
HMS *Swift*	Force D
HMS *Talybont*	Force C
HMS *Tanatside*	Force C
HMS *Tartar*	10th Destroyer Flotilla
USS *Thompson*	Force C Western Force Flagship Group
HMS *Ulster*	Force K
HMS *Ulysses*	Force K
HMS *Undaunted*	Force K
HMS *Undine*	Force K
HMS *Urania*	Force K
HMS *Urchin*	Force K
HMS *Ursa*	Force K
HMS *Venus*	Force E
HMS *Versatile*	Force J
HMS *Verulam*	Force D
HMS *Vesper*	Force O
HMS *Vidette*	Force O
HMS *Vigilant*	Force E
HMS *Vimy*	Force B
HMS *Virago*	Force D

HMS *Vivacious*	Force L
HMS *Volunteer*	Force B
USS *Walker*	Escort vessel Utah beach
HMS *Wensleydale*	Western Task Force
HMS *Wrestler*	Eastern Task Force (damaged by mines)

OTHER DESTROYERS ENGAGED IN OPERATION NEPTUNE

HMS *Duff*	HMS *Onslow*
HMS *Endicott*	HMS *Opportune*
HMS *Hotham*	HMS *Oribi*
HMS *Isis*	HMS *Orwell*
HMS *Obedient*	HMS *Savage*
HMS *Offa*	HMS *Westcott*
HMS *Onslaught*	

X CRAFT (Midget submarines used as navigational beacons)

X *20*	(Lieutenant K. Hudspeth RN) Juno beach
X *23*	(Lieutenant G. Honour RNVR) Sword beach

SLOOPS

HNMS *Flores*	Force K - Royal Netherlands Navy
HMS *Hind*	Gold beach
HMS *Magpie*	Gold beach
HMS *Redpole*	Gold beach
HNMS *Soemba*	Force A
HMS *Stork*	Sword beach

CORVETTES

FFS *Aconit*	Western Task Force
HMS *Alberni*	Eastern Task Force

HMS *Armeria*	Eastern Task Force
HMS *Azalea*	Western Task Force
HMS *Bluebell*	Western Task Force
HMS *Boadicea*	Escort vessel Western Task Force (sunk)
HMS *Campanula*	Eastern Task Force
HMS *Clarkia*	Eastern Task Force
HMS *Clematis*	Eastern Task Force
HMS *Clover*	Eastern Task Force
HMS *Godetia*	Eastern Task Force
HMS *Kitchener*	Western Task Force
RHS *Kriezis*	Eastern Task Force - Royal Hellenic Navy
HMS *Lavender*	Eastern Task Force
HMS *Mignonette*	Eastern Task Force
HMS *Minico*	Eastern Task Force
HMS *Narcissus*	Eastern Task Force
HMS *Oxslip*	Eastern Task Force
HMS *Pennywort*	Eastern Task Force
HMS *Petunia*	Eastern Task Force
FFS *Renoncule*	Western Task Force
RHS *Tompazis*	Eastern Task Force

FRIGATES

FFS *Aventure*	Western Task Force
HMS *Chelmer*	Force L
FFS *Commandant Etienne d'Orve*	Eastern Task Force Gold beach
HMS *Dacres*	Eastern Task Force
FFS *Découverte*	Eastern Task Force
FFS *Escarmouche*	Western Task Force
HMS *Halsted*	Force L (torpedoed)
HMS *Holmes*	Force D
HMS *Kingsmill*	Eastern Task Force
HMS *Lawford*	Eastern Task Force (sunk)
HMS *Nith*	Eastern Task Force
FFS *Roselys*	Western Task Force

HMS *Rowley*	Force D
FFS *Surprise*	Eastern Task Force
HMS *Torrington*	Eastern Task Force
HMS *Waveny*	Eastern Task Force

OTHER FRIGATES ENGAGED IN OPERATION NEPTUNE

HMS *Retalick*
HMS *Riou*
HMS *Stayner*
HMS *Thornborough*
HMS *Trollope* (torpedoed)

MONITORS

HMS *Erebus*	Force A
HMS *Roberts*	Force D

MINESWEEPERS

HMS *Albury*	Western Task Force
USS *Auk*	Western Task Force
HMS *Beaumarais*	Western Task Force
HMCS *Blairmore*	Western Task Force
USS *Broadbill*	Western Task Force
HMCS *Caraquet*	Western Task Force
HMS *Catherine*	Eastern Task Force
USS *Chickadee*	Western Task Force
HMCS *Cowichan*	Western Task Force
HMS *Dornock*	Western Task Force
HMCS *Fort William*	Western Task Force
HMS *Fraserburgh*	Eastern Task Force
HMS *Guysborough*	Western Task Force
HMS *Harrier*	Eastern Task Force
HMS *Ilfracombe*	Western Task Force
HMS *Kellet*	Western Task Force

HMS *Kenova*	Western Task Force
HMS *Lydd*	Western Task Force
HMCS *Malpèque*	Western Task Force
HMCS *Minas*	Western Task Force
HMCS *Mulgrave*	Western Task Force
USS *Nuthatch*	Western Task Force
USS *Osprey*	Western Task Force (sunk)
HMS *Pangbourne*	Western Task Force
HMS *Parrsboro*	Western Task Force
HMS *Pelorous*	Eastern Task Force
USS *Pheasant*	Eastern Task Force
HMS *Poole*	Western Task Force
HMS *Qualicum*	Western Task Force
USS *Raven*	Western Task Force
HMS *Ready*	Eastern Task Force
HMS *Romney*	Western Task Force
HMS *Ross*	Western Task Force
HMS *Rye*	Western Task Force
HMS *Saltash*	Western Task Force
HMS *Seaham*	Western Task Force
HMS *Selkirk*	Western Task Force
HMS *Shippigan*	Western Task Force
HMS *Sidmouth*	Eastern Task Force
USS *Staff*	Western Task Force
HMS *Sutton*	Western Task Force
USS *Swift*	Western Task Force (sunk)
HMS *Tadoussac*	Western Task Force
USS *Threat*	Western Task Force
HMS *Thunder*	Western Task Force
USS *Tide*	Western Task Force (sunk)
HMCS *Vegreville*	Western Task Force
HMS *Vestal*	Eastern Task Force
HMCS *Wasaga*	Western Task Force
HMS *Wedgeport*	Western Task Force
HMS *Whitehaven*	Western Task Force

OTHER MINESWEEPERS ENGAGED IN NEPTUNE

HMS *Ardrossan*
HMS *Bangor*
HMS *Blackpool*
HMS *Bootle*
HMS *Boston*
HMS *Bridlington*
HMS *Bridport*
HMS *Britomart*
HMS *Cato*
HMS *Cockatrice*
HMS *Dunbar*
HMS *Eastbourne*
HMS *Elgin*
HMS *Fancy*
HMS *Fort York*
HMS *Friendship*
HMS *Gazelle*
HMS *Georgian*
HMS *Gleaner*
HMS *Gorgon*
HMS *Gozo*
HMS *Grecian*
HMS *Halcyon*
HMS *Hound*
HMS *Hussar*
HMS *Hydra*

HMS *Jason*
HMS *Larne*
HMS *Lennox*
HMS *Llandudno*
HMS *Loyalty*
HMS *Lyme Regis*
HMS *Melita*
HMS *Milltown*
HMS *Onyx*
HMS *Orestes*
HMS *Persian*
HMS *Pickle*
HMS *Pincher*
HMS *Pique*
HMS *Plucky*
HMS *Postillion*
HMS *Rattlesnake*
HMS *Recruit*
HMS *Rifleman*
HMS *Salamander*
HMS *Seagull*
HMS *Speedwell*
HMS *Steadfast*
HMS *Tenby*
HMS *Worthing*

ASDIC TRAWLERS

HMS *Bombardier*
HMS *Bressay*
HMS *Coll*
HMS *Cornelian*
HMS *Damsay*
HMS *Ellesmere*
HMS *Fiaray*

HMS *Lord Austin*
HMS *Northern Foam*
HMS *Northern Gift*
HMS *Northern Pride*
HMS *Northern Reward*
HMS *Northern Sky*
HMS *Northern Spray*

HMS *Flint*	HMS *Northern Sun*
HMS *Foulness*	HMS *Northern Wave*
HMS *Fusilier*	HMS *Olivina*
HMS *Gairsay*	HMS *Pearl*
HMS *Gateshead*	HMS *Sapper*
HMS *Grenadier*	HMS *Skye*
HMS *Hugh Walpole*	HMS *Texada*
HMS *Lancer*	HMS *Veleta*
HMS *Lindisfarne*	HMS *Victrix*

SUBMARINE CHASERS

FFS *Audierne*	Escort to Gold beach
FFS *Calais*	Escort to Gold beach
FFS *Dielette*	Escort to Gold beach
FFS *Paimpol*	Escort to Gold beach

SALVAGE, TUGS, REPAIR AND RESCUE SHIPS

HMS *Abigail*	Western Task Force
HMS *Admiral Sir John Lawford*	Western Task Force
USS *Adonis*	Western Task Force
USS *Arikara*	Western Task Force
USS *Bannock*	Western Task Force
USS *Brant*	Western Task Force
USS *Diver*	Western Task Force
USS *Eleazer Wheelock*	Western Task Force Far Shore Service
HMS *Help*	Western Task Force
USS *Kiowa*	Western Task Force
HMS *Marie*	Western Task Force
HMS *Partridge*	Western Task Force (sunk)
USS *Pinto*	Western Task Force
HMS *Sesame*	Western Task Force (sunk)
USS *Swivel*	Western Task Force
HMS *Tehana*	Western Task Force

LANDING SHIPS HEADQUARTERS

HMS *Locust*   Eastern Task Force
HMS *Royal Ulsterman*   Eastern Task Force

LANDING SHIPS ENGINEER

HMS *Adventure*   Force G
HMS *Albatross*   Force S

LANDING SHIPS DOCK - LS(D)

HMS *Northway*
HMS *Oceanway*

LANDING SHIPS TANK

HMS *Bachaquero*
HMS *Misoa*
HMS *Tasajera*

In addition to the above named ships, there were 174 Landing Ships Tank used by the US Navy and 59 by the Royal Navy. These were numbered and not named and were a smaller capacity than the three named above.

LANDING SHIPS INFANTRY

SS *Amsterdam*	HMS *Invicta*
HMS *Ben-My-Chree*	HMS *Isle of Guernsey*
SS *Biarritz*	HMS *Isle of Thanet*
HMS *Brigadier*	SS *Lady of Man*
SS *Canterbury*	SS *Laird's Isle*
SS *Clan Lamont*	HMS *Llangibby Castle*
SS *Duke of Argyll*	SS *Maid of Orleans*

SS *Duke of Wellington*
HMS *Empire Anvil*
HMS *Empire Arquebus*
HMS *Empire Battleaxe*
HMS *Empire Broadsword*
HMS *Empire Crossbow*
HMS *Empire Cutlass*
HMS *Empire Gauntlet*
HMS *Empire Halberd*
HMS *Empire Javelin*
HMS *Empire Lance*
HMS *Empire Mace*
HMS *Empire Rapier*
HMS *Empire Spearhead*
HMS *Glen Farn*
HMS *Glen Roy*

SS *Mecklenburg*
SS *Monowai*
HMS *Prince Baudouin*
HMS *Prince Charles*
HMCS *Prince David*
HMCS *Prince Henry*
HMS *Prince Leopold*
SS *Princess Astrid*
SS *Princess Margaret*
SS *Princess Maud*
SS *Princess Victoria*
HMS *Queen Emma*
HMS *Royal Ulsterman*
HMS *St Helier*
HMS *Ulster Monarch*

ATTACK FREIGHTERS AND TRANSPORTS

USS *Ann Arundell*
USS *Achernar*
USS *Barnett*
HMS *Brackenfield* (sunk)
USS *Charles Carroll*
HMS *Dungrange* (sunk)
USS *Samuel Chase*

USS *Joseph T. Dickman*
HMS *Iddesleigh*
USS *Dorothea L. Dix*
USS *Henrico*
USS *Thomas Jefferson*
USS *Thurston*

LANDING SHIPS AND LANDING CRAFT TYPES

The armada engaged in putting ashore the land forces in Operation Overlord totalled 4,126 vessels. The Royal Navy provided 3,261 while the US Navy and US Coastguard had 865 under the American flag.

The following is a listing of the types of ship and small craft under their designations.

LSC *Landing Ship Carrier*, used for ferrying Landing Craft. Three versions were in service:
LSD *Landing Ship Dock*, carrying either 3 LCTs or 14 LCAs.
LSG *Landing Ship Gantry*
LSS *Landing Ship Stern-chute*

LSH *Landing Ship Headquarters*. These were converted armed merchant cruisers and passenger liners, as command posts for commanders of all services, equipped with operations rooms, radio communication and accommodation for staff. They also conveyed troops employed in the landings who went ashore in *Landing Craft Personnel* (LCP) carried on the ships' davits. All five ships were named and are listed under 'Headquarters Ships' above. (2 in Western and 3 in Eastern Task Forces).

LSI *Landing Ship Infantry*. This was the designation applied to passenger and cargo merchant ships converted to carry a large number of men (up to about 700) and up to twelve LCAs in place of lifeboats. (18 in Western and 37 in Eastern Task Forces).

LSK *Landing Ship Kitchen*. Converted and equipped to provide hot meals. Carried provisions for 900 men for seven days.

LST *Landing Ship Tank*. Ocean-going vessels with bow doors and ramps. LSTs were either beached while at anchor into LCTs or Rhino Ferries. Some LSTs were used as Flight Direction ships, carrying RAF radar equipment. After D-Day some LSTs were converted to carry railway locomotives and rolling stock. (106 in Western and 130 in Eastern Task Forces).

LCA *Landing Craft Assault*. Armoured craft with capacity of 800 lbs equipment and 36 men who landed by means of a ramp in the bow.

LCA(H) *Landing Craft Assault (Hedgerow)*. Armament: twenty-four 60 lbs Spigot bombs. (45 in Eastern Task Force).

LCF *Landing Craft Flak*. Armament: four two-pounders and

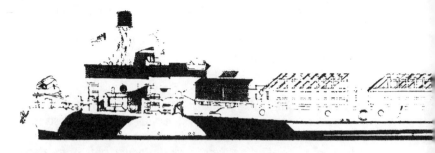

four or eight 20mm Oerlikon guns. (11 in Western and 18 in Eastern Task Forces).

LCG *Landing Craft Gun.* Armament: two 4.7" naval guns and between two and seven 20mm Oerlikon AA guns or two 4.7" naval guns and two two-pounders. (9 in Western and 16 in Eastern Task Forces).

LCI(S) *Landing Craft Infantry (Small).* Wooden-hulled with a capacity of 102 men and 18 bicycles. (39 in Eastern Task Force).

LCI(L) *Landing Craft Infantry (Large).* Capacity of 188 men or 75 tons cargo. (93 in Western and 116 in Eastern Task Force).

LCM *Landing Craft Mechanised.* A craft capable of carrying an 18-ton tank but light enough to be lifted out of the water by ship's derricks.

LCN *Landing Craft Navigational.* Small craft fitted with beacon and navigational equipment.

LCVP *Landing Craft Vehicle and Personnel.* Unarmoured craft with bow ramp. US built version of British design.

LCP *Landing Craft Personnel.* Similar to LCVP but without bow ramp.

LCS(L) *Landing Craft Support (Large).* Armament: one six-

LCT(R) *Landing Craft Tank (Rocket)*

pounder or two-pounder gun mounted in a tank turret, two 20mm Oerlikon AA guns, one 4" smoke mortar and machine guns. (14 in Eastern Task Force).

LCS(M) *Landing Craft Support (Medium)*. Armament: one 4" smoke mortar and machine guns. (2 in Western and 24 in Eastern Task Forces).

LCS(S) *Landing Craft Support (Small)*. Armament: twenty-four rockets and machine guns. (36 in Western Task Force).

LCT *Landing Craft Tank*. Flat-bottomed with a drop bow-ramp to discharge between four and six tanks or other vehicles. Built in two sizes: LCT(1) and LCT(2). (26 in Western and 103 in Eastern Task Forces).

LCT(R) *Landing Craft Tank (Rocket)*. Armament: up to 1,064 5" High Explosive rockets. (14 in Western and 22 in Eastern Task Forces).

LCT (T) *Landing Craft Tank* with temporary mounted armament: Centaur tanks with 96mm howitzers or Sherman tanks with 75mm guns or self-propelled field guns or seventeen-pounder high velocity guns for use against concrete defences. (26 in Western and 103 in Eastern Task Forces).

Rhino Ferry. Raft made up from steel pontoons and driven by a datachable propulsion unit. (31 in Western and 41 in Eastern Task Forces).

ALLIED NAVAL LOSSES

By shore fire and air attack:
HMS *Boadicea*
USS *Glennon*
HMS *Lawford*
USS *Meredith* (Damaged beyond repair)
FFS *Mistral* (Damaged beyond repair)

By mines:
USS *Corry*
USS *Osprey*
USS *Rich*
USS *Tide*
USS *Wrestler*

By torpedo-boat:
HNMS *Svenner*

By S-Boat:
USS *Nelson*
3 Freighters
1 Landing Craft, Infantry
2 Landing Craft, Tank
1 Landing Ship, Infantry
4 Landing Ships, Tank
1 Motor Torpedo Boat
1 Tug

Targets of the Naval Bombardment Forces at 05.30 - 08.00 hours on D-Day, showing the position of forces and naval vessels. >

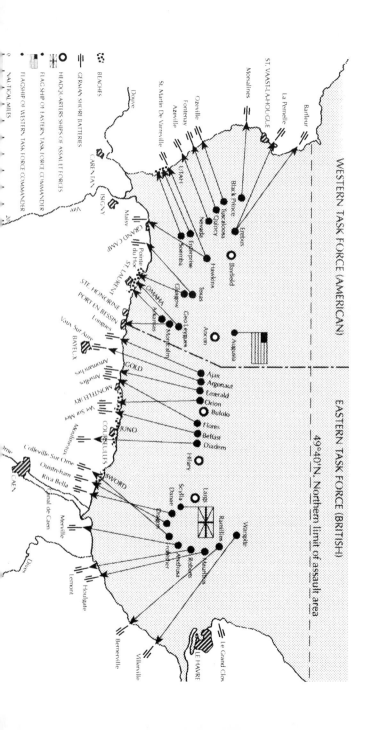

VI ALLIED AIR FORCES

(Air Chief Marshal Trafford Leigh Mallory)

ROYAL AIR FORCE. SECOND TACTICAL AIR FORCE formed on 1st June 1943 specifically for Operation OVERLORD (Air Marshal Arthur Coningham)

34 RECONNAISSANCE WING

16 Squadron	*Spitfire,*
69 Squadron	*Wellington* and
140 Squadron	*Mosquito*

3 NAVAL FIGHTER WING (Air Spotting Pool)

808 (Fleet Air Arm) Squadron	
885 (Fleet Air Arm) Squadron	
886 (Fleet Air Arm) Squadron	
847 (Fleet Air Arm) Squadron	*Seafire F111*
26 Squadron	
63 Squadron	*Spitfire LVB*
1320 Special Duty Flight	*Typhoon*
VCS-7 Unit comprising 17 US Navy pilots, under Commander E. C. Thornton RN	*Spitfire*

No 2 GROUP BOMBER COMMAND
(Air Vice Marshal B. E. Embry)

137 WING

88 Squadron	
226 Squadron	
342 (French) Squadron	*Mitchell*

138 WING

107 Squadron
305 (Polish) Squadron
615 Squadron — *Mitchell*

139 WING

98 Squadron
180 Squadron
320 (Dutch) Squadron — *Mitchell*

140 WING

21 Squadron
464 (RAAF) Squadron
487 (RNZAF) Squadron — *Mosquito*

No 85 (COMPOSITE) GROUP
(Air Vice-Marshal H. Broadhurst)

39 (RCAF) Squadron
168 Squadron
400 (RCAF) Squadron
414 (RCAF) Squadron — *Mustang*

RECONNAISSANCE WING

430 (RCAF) Squadron — *Spitfire*

121 WING

174 Squadron
175 Squadron
245 Squadron — *Typhoon*

122 WING

- 19 Squadron
- 65 Squadron
- 122 Squadron — *Mustang*

124 WING

- 181 Squadron
- 182 Squadron
- 247 Squadron — *Typhoon*

125 WING

- 132 Squadron
- 453 (RAAF) Squadron
- 602 Squadron — *Spitfire*

126 (RCAF) WING

- 401 (RCAF) Squadron
- 411 (RCAF) Squadron
- 412 (RCAF) Squadron — *Spitfire*

127 (RCAF) WING

- 403 (RCAF) Squadron
- 416 (RCAF) Squadron
- 421 (RCAF) Squadron — *Spitfire*

129 (RCAF) WING

- 184 Squadron — *Typhoon*

143 (RCAF) WING

- 438 (RCAF) Squadron
- 439 (RCAF) Squadron
- 440 (RCAF) Squadron — *Typhoon*

144 (RCAF) WING

441 (RCAF) Squadron
442 (RCAF) Squadron
443 (RCAF) Squadron — *Spitfire*

AIR OBSERVATION POSTS

652 Squadron
653 Squadron
658 Squadron
659 Squadron
662 Squadron — *Auster*

No 84 (COMPOSITE) GROUP
(Air Vice-Marshal L. O. Brown)

35 RECONNAISSANCE WING

2 Squadron
4 Squadron
268 Squadron — *Mustang F6* and *Spitfire*

123 WING

198 Squadron
609 Squadron — *Typhoon*

131 (POLISH) WING

302 (Polish) Squadron
308 (Polish) Squadron
317 (Polish) Squadron — *Spitfire*

132 (NORWEGIAN) WING

66 Squadron
331 (Norwegian) Squadron
332 (Norwegian) Squadron ⌐ *Spitfire*

133 (POLISH) WING

129 Squadron
306 (Polish) Squadron
315 (Polish) Squadron ⌐ *Mustang*

134 (CZECHOSLOVAKIAN) WING

310 (Czechoslovakian) Squadron
312 (Czechoslovakian) Squadron
313 (Czechoslovakian) Squadron ⌐ *Spitfire*

135 WING

222 Squadron
349 (Belgian) Squadron
485 (RNZAF) Squadron ⌐ *Spitfire*

136 WING

164 Squadron
183 Squadron ⌐ *Typhoon*

145 (FRENCH) WING

329 (French) Squadron
340 (French) Squadron
341 (French) Squadron ⌐ *Spitfire*

146 WING

193 Squadron
197 Squadron
257 Squadron
266 Squadron — *Typhoon*

AIR OBSERVATION POSTS

660 Squadron
661 Squadron — *Auster*

No 85 (BASE) GROUP

141 WING

91 Squadron
124 Squadron
322 (Dutch) Squadron — *Spitfire*

142 WING

246 Squadron
604 Squadron — *Mosquito Night Fighter*

147 WING

29 Squadron — *Mosquito Night Fighter*

148 WING

409 (RCAF) Squadron — *Mosquito Night Fighter*

149 WING

410 (RCAF) Squadron   *Mosquito*
488 (RNZAF) Squadron   *Night Fighter*

150 WING

56 Squadron   *Spitfire and Tempest*

3 Squadron
486 (RNZAF) Squadron   *Tempest*

AIRFIELD CONSTRUCTION WING

5022 Squadron
5023 Squadron
5357 Squadron

BEACH SQUADRONS

1 Beach Squadron
2 Beach Squadron
4 Beach Squadron

No 15083 GROUND CONTROL INTERCEPTION UNIT

BALLOON SQUADRONS

974 Balloon Squadron
976 Balloon Squadron
980 Balloon Squadron
991 Balloon Squadron
104 Port Balloon Flight

ROYAL AIR FORCE REGIMENT GROUP
(Colonel R. L. Preston)

MOBILE WINGS

1300, 1301, 1302, 1303, 1304, 1305, 1306, 1307, 1308, 1309, 1310, 1311, 1312, 1314, 1315, 1316, 1317 and 1318

ARMOURED SQUADRONS

2742, 2757, 2777, 2781, 2806 and 2817

LIGHT ANTI-AIRCRAFT SQUADRONS

2701, 2703, 2734, 2736, 2773, 2794, 2800, 2809, 2819, 2834, 2843, 2872, 2873, 2874, 2875, 2876, 2880 and 2881

RIFLE SQUADRONS

2713, 2717, 2726, 2729, 2798, 2816 and 2827
2739 Special Duty Squadron

ROYAL AIR FORCE AIR DEFENCE OF GREAT BRITAIN
formerly Fighter Command
(Air Marshal Roderic Hill)

No 10 GROUP
(Air Vice-Marshal C. R. Steele)

1 Squadron	
41 Squadron	
126 Squadron	
131 Squadron	*Spitfire*
165 Squadron	
610 Squadron	
612 Squadron	
263 Squadron	*Typhoon*

151 Squadron	Mosquito N. F.
68 Squadron	Beaufighter
406 (RCAF) Squadron	Night Fighter
276 (Air-Sea Rescue) Squadron	Spitfire, Warwick and Walrus
1449 Flight	Hurricane

No 11 GROUP
(Air Vice-Marshal H. W. L. Saunders)

33 Squadron	
64 Squadron	
74 Squadron	
80 Squadron	
127 Squadron	
130 Squadron	
229 Squadron	
234 Squadron	
274 Squadron	
303 (Polish) Squadron	
345 (French) Squadron	
250 (Belgian) Squadron	
402 (RCAF) Squadron	
501 Squadron	
611 Squadron	Spitfire
137 Squadron	Typhoon
96 Squadron	
125 (Newfoundland) Squadron	
229 Squadron	Mosquito
456 (RAAF) Squadron	Night Fighter
418 (RCAF) Squadron	Mosquito and Intruder
275 (Air-Sea Rescue) Squadron	Spitfire,
277 (Air-Sea Rescue) Squadron	Warwick
278 (Air-Sea Rescue) Squadron	and Walrus

No 12 GROUP
(Air Vice-Marshal M. Henderson)

316 (Polish) Squadron	Mustang
504 Squadron	Spitfire
25 Squadron	Mosquito
307 (Polish) Squadron	Night Fighter
Flight Interception Unit	Beaufighter, Mosquito, Mustang and Tempest

No 13 GROUP
(Air Commodore J. A. Boret)

118 Squadron	Spitfire
309 (Polish) Squadron	Hurricane

Air Defence of Great Britain included Ground-Based Air Defences.

ROYAL AIR FORCE AIRBORNE AND TRANSPORT FORCES

No 38 GROUP - AIRBORNE FORCES
(Air Vice-Marshal L. N. Hollinghurst)

295 Squadron	
296 Squadron	
297 Squadron	
570 Squadron	Albermarle
190 Squadron	
196 Squadron	
299 Squadron	
620 Squadron	Stirling
298 Squadron	
644 Squadron	Halifax

No 46 GROUP TRANSPORT COMMAND
(Air Vice-Marshal A. L. Fiddament)

48 Squadron
233 Squadron
271 Squadron
512 Squadron
575 Squadron   *Dakota*

UNITED STATES NINTH AIR FORCE
Formed in the Middle East in November 1943 and moved to England in September 1943.
(Major-General Lewis H. Brereton).

In US Air Forces, Wings were equivalent to RAF Groups and Groups equivalent to Wings.

IX TACTICAL AIR COMMAND
(Major-General Elwood R. Quesada, also commander of IX Fighter Command)

70 WING, 12 squadrons in 4 groups

48 Group
367 Group
371 Group   *Lightning*
474 Group   and *Thunderbolt*

71 WING, 9 squadrons in 3 groups

366 Group
368 Group   *Lightning*
370 Group   and *Thunderbolt*

84 WING, 16 squadrons in 5 groups

50 Group
365 Group
404 Group
405 Group — *Thunderbolt*
67 Tactical Reconnaissance Group — *Mustang*

IX BOMBER COMMAND
(Brigadier-General Samuel E. Anderson)

97 WING, 45 squadrons in 11 groups

409 Group
410 Group
416 Group — *Havoc*

98 WING

323 Group
387 Group
394 Group
397 Group — *Marauder*

99 WING

322 Group
344 Group
386 Group
391 Group
One Pathfinder Squadron — *Marauder*

IX TROOP CARRIER COMMAND
(Brigadier-General Paul L. Williams)

50 WING

439 Group
440 Group
441 Group
442 Group — *Dakota*

52 WING

61 Group
313 Group
314 Group
315 Group
316 Group — *Dakota*

53 WING

434 Group
435 Group
436 Group
437 Group
438 Group — *Dakota*
One Pathfinder Group

IX AIR DEFENCE COMMAND
(Brigadier-General William L. Richardson)

IX AIR FORCE SERVICE COMMAND
(Brigadier-General Myron Wood)

IX ENGINEER COMMAND
(Brigadier-General James Newman)

ALLIED STRATEGIC AIR FORCES

ROYAL AIR FORCE BOMBER COMMAND

No 1 GROUP
(Air Vice-Marshal E. A. B. Rice)

12 Squadron
100 Squadron
101 Squadron
103 Squadron
166 Squadron
300 (Polish) Squadron
550 Squadron
576 Squadron
625 Squadron
626 Squadron — *Lancaster*

No 3 GROUP
(Air Vice-Marshal R. Harrison)

15 Squadron
75 Squadron
115 Squadron
514 Squadron
622 Squadron — *Lancaster*
90 Squadron — *Lacaster* and *Stirling*

149 Squadron
218 Squadron — *Stirling*
138 Special Duty Squadron — *Halifax* and *Stirling*

161 Special Duty Squadron — *Halifax, Hudson* and *Lysander*

No 4 GROUP
(Air Vice-Marshal C. R. Carr)

10 Squadron
51 Squadron
76 Squadron
77 Squadron
78 Squadron
102 Squadron
158 Squadron
346 (French) Squadron
347 (French) Squadron
462 (RAAF) Squadron
466 (RAAF) Squadron
578 Squadron
640 Squadron — *Halifax*

No 5 GROUP
(Air Vice-Marshal The Hon R. A. Cochrane)

9 Squadron
44 (Rhodesian) Squadron
49 Squadron
50 Squadron
57 Squadron
61 Squadron
106 Squadron
207 Squadron
463 (RAAF) Squadron
467 (RAAF) Squadron
619 Squadron
630 Squadron — *Lancaster*
617 Squadron — *Lancaster and Mosquito*

No 6 (ROYAL CANADIAN AIR FORCE) GROUP
(Air Vice-Marshal C. M. McEwen RCAF)

420 (RCAF) Squadron	
424 (RCAF) Squadron	
425 (RCAF) Squadron	
426 (RCAF) Squadron	
427 (RCAF) Squadron	
429 (RCAF) Squadron	
431 (RCAF) Squadron	
432 (RCAF) Squadron	
433 (RCAF) Squadron	
434 (RCAF) Squadron	*Halifax*
408 (RCAF) Squadron	
419 (RCAF) Squadron	*Lancaster*
428 (RCAF) Squadron	*Halifax and Lancaster*

No 8 PATHFINDER GROUP
(Air Vice-Marshal D. C. T. Bennett)

7 Squadron	
35 Squadron	
83 Squadron	
97 Squadron	
156 Squadron	
405 (RCAF) Squadron	
582 Squadron	
635 Squadron	*Lancaster*
105 Squadron	
109 Squadron	
139 Squadron	
571 Squadron	
608 Squadron	
627 Squadron	
692 Squadron	*Mosquito*

No 100 (BOMBER SUPPORT) GROUP
(Air Commodore E. B. Addison)

85 (Bomber Support) Squadron	
141 (Bomber Support) Squadron	
157 (Bomber Support) Squadron	
169 (Bomber Support) Squadron	
239 (Bomber Support) Squadron	*Mosquito*
23 (Bomber Support) Squadron	*Mosquito* and *Intruder*
515 (Bomber Support) Squadron	
214 (Bomber Support) Squadron	*Fortress*
192 (Bomber Support) Squadron	*Mosquito* and *Wellington*
199 Squadron	*Stirling*

UNITED STATES EIGHTH AIR FORCE
Formed in January 1942 at Savannah, Georgia.
(Lieutenant General James Doolittle)

7 Photographic Reconnaissance Group *Lightning* and *Spitfire*
(4 squadrons)

1st BOMB DIVISION
(Major-General Robert B. Williams) 48 squadrons in 12 groups

91 Group	
92 Group	
303 Group	
305 Group	
306 Group	
351 Group	
379 Group	
381 Group	
384 Group	
398 Group	
401 Group	
457 Group	*Fortress*

2nd BOMB DIVISION
(Major-General James P. Hodges) 56 squadrons in 14 groups

44 Group
93 Group
389 Group
392 Group
445 Group
446 Group
448 Group
453 Group
458 Group
466 Group
467 Group
489 Group
491 Group
492 Group — *Liberator*

3rd BOMB DIVISION
(Major-General Curtis E. Le May) 56 squadrons in 14 groups

94 Group
95 Group
96 Group
100 Group
385 Group
388 Group
390 Group
447 Group
452 Group — *Fortress*
34 Group
486 Group
487 Group
490 Group
493 Group — *Liberator*

VIII FIGHTER COMMAND
(Major-General William E. Kepner) 45 squadrons in 15 groups

65 WING

4 Group
56 Group
355 Group — *Lightning,*
356 Group — *Mustang*
479 Group — and *Thunderbolt*

66 WING

55 Group
78 Group
339 Group — *Lightning,*
353 Group — *Mustang*
357 Group — and *Thunderbolt*

67 WING

20 Group
352 Group
359 Group
361 Group — *Lightning*
364 Group — and *Mustang*

Detachment B - 5th Emergency Rescue Squadron

VIII AIR FORCE SERVICE COMMAND
(Colonel Donald R. Goodrich)

VIII AIR FORCE COMPOSITE COMMAND

8th RECONNAISSANCE WING (PROVISIONAL)

ROYAL AIR FORCE COASTAL COMMAND
(Air Chief Marshal W. Sholto Douglas)

No 15 GROUP
(Air Vice-Marshal Sir Leonard H. Slatter)

59 Squadron	*Liberator* (very long range)
120 Squadron	*Liberator* (v. l. r. with Leigh Light)
422 (RCAF) Squadron	
423 (RCAF) Squadron	*Sunderland*
811 (Fleet Air Arm) Squadron	*Wild Cat*

No 16 GROUP
(Air Vice-Marshal F. L. Hope)

119 Squadron	*Albacore*
143 Squadron	
236 Squadron	
254 Squadron	
455 (RAAF) Squadron	
489 (RNZAF) Squadron	*Beaufighter*
415 (RCAF) Squadron	*Wellington* and *Albacore*
819 (Fleet Air Arm) Squadron	
848 (Fleet Air Arm) Squadron	
854 (Fleet Air Arm) Squadron	*Avenger*
855 (Fleet Air Arm) Squadron	and *Swordfish*

No 18 GROUP
(Air Vice-Marshal S. P. Simpson)

86 Squadron	*Liberator* (v. l. r.)

210 Squadron	⌐ *Catalina*
330 (Norwegian) Squadron	│ *Mosquito*
333 (Norwegian) Squadron	⌐ and *Sunderland*
1693 Flight	⌐ *Anson*

No 19 GROUP
(Air Vice-Marshal B. E. Baker)

144 Squadron	
235 Squadron	
404 (RCAF) Squadron	⌐ *Beaufighter*
58 Squadron	
502 Squadron	⌐ *Halifax*
53 Squadron	│ *Liberator* fitted
224 Squadron	⌐ with Leigh Light
206 Squadron	
311 (Czechoslovakian) Squadron	
547 Squadron	⌐ *Liberator*
248 Squadron	⌐ *Mosquito*
10 (RAAF) Squadron	
201 Squadron	
228 Squadron	
461 (RAAF) Squadron	⌐ *Sunderland*
172 Squadron	
179 Squadron	
304 (Polish) Squadron	
407 (RCAF) Squadron	*Wellington XIV*
612 Squadron	⌐ with Leigh Light
524 Squadron	⌐ *Wellington*
816 (Fleet Air Arm) Squadron	
838 (Fleet Air Arm) Squadron	
849 (Fleet Air Arm) Squadron	*Avenger*
850 (Fleet Air Arm) Squadron	⌐ and *Swordfish*
103 Squadron (US Navy attached)	
105 Squadron (US Navy attached)	
110 Squadron (US Navy attached)	
114 Squadron (US Navy attached)	⌐ *Liberator*

VII THE FRENCH RESISTANCE

There were numerous organisations in France undermining the German occupation with acts of sabotage, and otherwise harassing the occupying forces. The largest and best known of these organisations was that of the French Forces of the Interior (FFI), also known as the Maquis - this is a Corsican word for the marshy country used by outlaws.

In Normandy there were many resistance groups affiliated to the FFI. Most of these had associations with other movements, among which were:

Organisation Civile et Militaire (OCM)
Organisation de Résistance de L'Armée (ORA)
Francs-Tireurs et Partisans (FTP) - a pro-Communist organisation.
Libération-Nord

It has been estimated that there were some 3,000 members of the Resistance in the departments of Calvados and Manche in Normandy at the time of D-Day, armed and supplied by airdrop from Britain. Supplies and orders for sabotage operations were co-ordinated from London by the Special Operations Executive (SOE) which transmitted directions through the Overseas Service of the British Broadcasting Corporation.

Members of the Resistance in Normandy were popularly known as *Scameroni* from the name of one of their leaders, a Corsican, who had been caught and tortured by the Gestapo. Throughout the interrogation he remained silent.

Early in 1944 the British SOE, Special Operations (SO) - a unit of the US Office of Strategic Services (OSS) - and the Free French headquarters in London, formed a special staff to supply the Resistance and co-ordinate sabotage activities in preparation for the forthcoming invasion. These operations included the dropping by parachute of variously-sized SO/SOE teams of officers and men into France, with, as their mission, the training and organisation of the Resistance.

After the Allied forces had landed, the activities of the Resistance accelerated, with the destruction of railway lines and locomotives and ambushing of German troops becoming vital in order to prevent reinforcements, ordnance and supplies reaching the combat areas. General Eisenhower, the Allied Supreme Commander, was later to say that the Resistance was worth between five and six divisions to him.

Once the invasion had started, the SO/SOE/FFI teams were supplemented by JEDBURGHS - teams comprising two officers (one Americans or British and the other French) and a radio operator - the teams' tasks were to collect intelligence behind enemy lines and to act as guides for the advancing Allied forces. In the first four months of the invasion there were no fewer than 87 Jedburghs and 18 French Special Air Service (SAS) teams operating in and behind the battle areas. Although naturally working in close association with the Resistance, these teams were quite separate. They wore uniform, or at least were expected to do so, and were under orders from the armies in the field.

VIII GERMAN COMMAND IN THE WEST

Supreme Commander of the Armed Forces
and Commander-in-Chief of the Army
Adolf Hitler

Armed Forces High Command (OKW)
Chief
Generalfeldmarschall Wilhelm Keitel

Chief of Operations Staff
Generaloberst Alfred Jodl

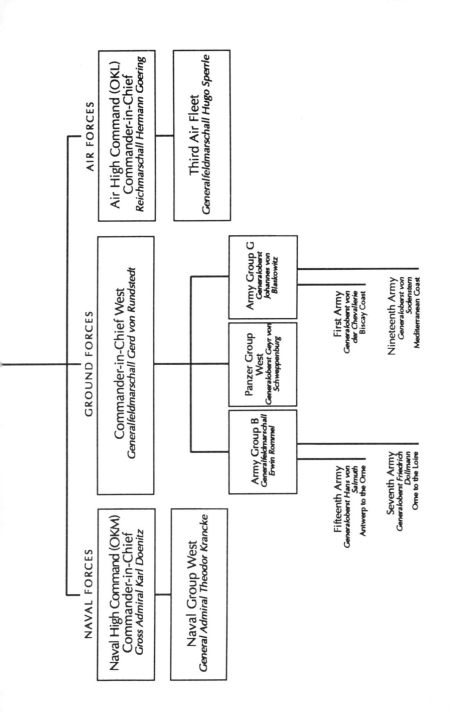

IX GERMAN WEHRMACHT FORCES

I SS PANZERKORPS
(General Joseph 'Sepp' Dietrich)

Corps headquarters moved from Brussels to Caen by evening of 6th June to take over th Caen area from LXXXIV Korps.

COMPONENT FORMATIONS OF I SS PANZERKORPS

12 SS PANZERDIVISION 'HITLERJUGEND'
(Gruppenführer Fritz Witt - killed in action 14th June)

The division's units were dispersed over a large area due east of Falaise, encompassing Bernay, Gureux, Dreux and Gace.

Divisional strength on D-Day:

20,500 all ranks
149 tanks (48 Panthers, 91 Mk IVs, 10 Jagdpanzer IVs)
333 armoured personnel carriers
52 artillery pieces
2,750 soft-skinned vehicles

By the evening of 6th June KAMPFGRUPPE MEYER, led by Sturmbannführer Kurt Meyer the commander of 25 Panzergrenadierregiment, was in action defending Carpiquet airfield west of Caen. Meyer's battle group consisted of II/915 Infanterieregiment and 352 Füsilierbataillon from 352 Infanteriedivision.

Units included 25 and 26 Panzergrenadierregimenten.

PANZER LEHR DIVISION
(Generalleutnant Fritz Bayerlein)

Divisional strength on D-Day:

189 tanks (Mk IVs, Panthers and some Tigers)
40 assault guns and Jagdpanzers
658 half-tracks

On D-Day this Division was based at Nogent-le-Rotron, eighty miles from the invasion beaches and did not reach the Caen area until late 8th June.

Units included 901 and 902 Panzergrenadier Lehr Regimenten.

21 PANZERDIVISION
(Generalmajor Edgar Feuchtinger)

This Division was in action on D-Day and was transferred to I SS Panzerkorps from LXXXIV Korps when Caen area was passed to the former.

Units included 100, 125 and 192 Panzergrenadierregimenten. The Division provided KAMPFGRUPPE LUCK, led by Oberst Hans von Luck, which delayed Allied advances north of Caen.

346 INFANTERIEDIVISION BODENSTANDIGE
(Generalleutnant Erick Diestel)

Headquarters were based at Le Havre on 6th June. The Division was involved in fighting with KAMPFGRUPPE LUCK (21 Panzerdivision) from 9th June.

Units included 858 Infanterieregiment and 744 Infanterieregiment transferred from 711 Infanteriedivision on 7th June.

716 INFANTERIEDIVISION BODENSTANDIGE (Generalmajor Wilhelm Richter)

Headquarters were based at St Lô on 6th June when the Division was transferred to I SS Panzerkorps from LXXXIV Korps.

Units included 726 and 736 Grenadierregimenten, and 1716 Artillerieregiment (formed from 656 Artillerieregiment). Elements from 21 Panzerdivision were attached.

The III/736 Grenadierregiment made a determined counter-attack against the British 3rd Infantry Division, retaking the village of Lion-sur-Mer on the eastern extremity of SWORD beach. By 9th June the Division had suffered so many casualties that it virtually ceased to exist.

LXXXIV KORPS
(General Erich Marcks - killed in action on 12th June. Corps then commanded by General Wilhelm Fahrmbacher until 15th June when he handed over to General Dietrich von Choltitz)

Headquarters were outside St Lô and the Corps' responsibility was the defence of a sector extending from Caen to the western side of the Contentin Peninsular. On 7th June the defence of the Caen area was transferred to I SS Panzerkorps, involving a change of command for the 21 Panzerdivision and the 716 Infanteriedivision Bodenstandige.

COMPONENT FORMATIONS OF LXXXIV KORPS

17 SS PANZERGRENADIERDIVISION 'GOTZ VON BERLICHINGEN'
(Gruppenführer Werner Ostendorff - wounded on 16th June and replaced by Standartenführer Otto Baum)

The Division was not in the invasion area on D-Day but was ordered from the South Loire and assigned to LXXXIV Korps. Advance parties reached the Carentan area on 11th June.

Units included 37 and 38 Grenadierregimenten. The 6 Fallschirmjägerregiment also came under the Division's command.

21 PANZERDIVISION
(Generalleutnant Edgar Feuchtinger)

Transferred to I SS Panzerkorps on 7th June.

77 INFANTERIEDIVISION
(Generalleutnant Rudolf Stegmann - killed in action on 18th June when command of the Division passed to Oberst Bernard Bacherer)

The Division was put on alert on D-Day but was not ordered into action. First engaged on 10th June at St Mère Eglise.

Units included 1049 and 1050 Grenadierregimenten and 177 Artillerieregiment.

Elements from this Division, together with the 243 Infanteriedivision, made up KAMPFGRUPPE HELLMICH from 10th June.

91 LUFTLANDEDIVISION
(Generalmajor Wilhelm Falley - killed in action at dawn on D-Day, leaving the Division leaderless and virtually ineffective. Command of remnants of the Division

was taken over by Oberst Bernard Klosterkemper on 18th June)

This was a Seventh Army reserve formation that came into early action against US Airborne forces, from which time it was taken under the command of LXXXIV Korps.

Units Included 1057 and 1058 Grenadierregimenten.

243 INFANTERIEDIVISION
(Generalleutnant Heinz Hellmich - killed in action on 17th June and succeeded by Oberstleutnant Franz Müller)

This Division was in action from the first landings by US Airborne forces.

Units included 921 and 922 Grenadierregimenten.
From 10th June KAMPFGRUPPE HELLMICH comprised the Division augmented by elements from the 77 Infanteriedivision.

275 INFANTERIEDIVISION
(Generalleutnant Hans Schmidt)

This Division was based in the St Lô area and was not suitably located for action on D-Day. KAMPFGRUPPE HEINZ (Kampfgruppe 275) reached the battle area on 13th June and was attached to the 17 SS Panzergrenadierdivision.

Units included 894, 895 and 896 Grenadierregimenten.

352 INFANTERIEDIVISION
(Generalleutnant Dietrich Kraiss)

In action on D-Day against both US and British forces in OMAHA and GOLD beach areas.

Units included 914, 916 and 726 Grenadierregimenten.

709 INFANTERIEDIVISION DODENSTANDIGE
(Generalleutnant Karl Wilhelm Schlieben)

In action on D-Day against US forces in UTAH area.

Units included 729 and 919 Grenadierregimenten. Georgian troops attached.

The Division ceased to exist on 30th June.

711 INFANTERIEDIVISION BODENSTANDIGE
(Generalleutnant Joseph Reichert)

In action against British 6th Airborne Division during night of 5th - 6th June.

Units included 731 Infanterieregiment and Russian troops. The Division's 744 Infanterieregiment was transferred to the 346 Infanteriedivision on 7th June.

716 INFANTERIEDIVISION BODENSTANDIGE
(Generalmajor Wilhelm Richter)

This Division was transferred to I SS Panzerkorps on 7th June.

WEHRMACHT FORMATIONS LATER ALLOCATED TO LXXXIV KORPS

Elements of 2 Panzerdivision.
3 Fallschirmjägerdivision.
6 Fallschirmjägerregiment.
Kampfgruppe 265 (from 265 Infanteriedivision).
752 Infanterieregiment.
319 Infanteriedivision Bodenstandige.

GERMAN ARMY ORGANISATION

The Panzer (Armoured) Divisions were fully motorised, but each had its individual establishment of vehicles and personnel.

The SS Panzer Divisions were of greater strength than their Wehrmacht counterparts, but all Panzer Divisions were composed of one Armoured Regiment (2 Battalions) and two Infantry Regiments (total of 4 Battalions for Wehrmacht and 6 Battalions for SS Divisions). In addition, Panzer Divisions included Reconnaissance, Artillery, Engineer and Signal Battalions. In the three or four Artillery Battalions a large proportion of the guns were self-propelled. Collectively, a Panzer Division would have about 160 tanks.

Manpower strength was about 15,000 but could be as much as 20,000 in some SS Divisions.

Panzer Grenadier Divisions were made up of a similar number of Infantry Battalions (4 for Wehrmacht and 6 for SS) and the total manpower strength was around 14,750.

Static Infantry Divisions and Parachute Divisions had nine Battalions of troops whereas the normal Infantry Divisions were composed of six Battalions. In most cases the Battalions were organised into three Regiments, each with its own Artillery. A Division also had a Fusilier Battalion generally used in a Reconnaissance role, as well as Artillery, Engineer, Signal and other supporting Battalions.

Manpower strength was about 12,500 all ranks.

SOME ENGLISH EQUIVALENTS FOR GERMAN RANKS AND FORMATIONS TITLES USED ABOVE

Bodenstandige - Non-mechanised
Fallschirmjägerdivision - Parachute Division
Fallschirmjägerregiment - Parachute Regiment
Generalleutnant - Major General
Generalmajor - Brigadier (British Army); Brigadier General (US Army)
Gruppenführer - Major General (SS rank)
Kampfgruppe - Battle Group
Oberst - Colonel
Oberstleutnant - Lieutenant Colonel
Panzer - Tank
Standartenführer - Colonel (SS rank)
Sturmbannführer - Major (SS rank)
Wehrmacht - Army

X GERMAN KRIEGSMARINE FORCES

In June 1944 Naval Group Command West (General Admiral Theodore Kranke) had the following numbers of vessels available for defensive operations:

DESTROYERS of 8 Flotilla, five in number only three of which were ready for service on 6th June.

TORPEDO BOATS of 4 and 5 Flotilla, six in number, only four of which were ready for service on 6th June.

S-BOATS (SCHNELLBOOTEN), forty-four in number, divided between 2 and 8 Flotillas based on Ostend, 4 Flotilla based on Boulogne, and 5 and 9 Flotillas based on Cherbourg. Of this total, twenty-nine vessels were operational on 6th June.

U-BOATS (UNTERWASSERBOOTEN) of Group Landwirt, forty-nine of which were stationed at the French Atlantic ports of Brest, Lorient, St Nazaire and La Palice. Thirty-five of this total had sailed before 2400 hours on 6th June.

For defence, the Western Defence Force (Konteradmiral Erich Alfred Breuning) had the following vessels available:

MINESWEEPERS (MINENSUCHBOOTEN), eighteen in number, divided between the Western Channel (2, 6 and 24 Flotillas) and the Bay of Biscay (8, 10, 26 and 28 Flotillas).

R-BOATS (RAUMBOOTEN) or motor minesweepers. Fifty-three in number, divided between 2 Flotilla based on Dunkirk, 4 Flotilla based on Dunkirk and Boulogne, 8 Flotilla based on Bruges, 10 Flotilla based on Le Havre, and 14 Flotilla based on Dieppe.

Large and medium-sized minesweepers (SPERRBRECHEREN).

Twenty-two in number, divided between 2 Flotilla based on Royan and 6 Flotilla based on Concarneau.

There were also numerous smaller craft used for minesweeping divided between 36 Flotilla based on Ostend, 38 Flotilla based on Le Harve, 40 and 46 Flotilla based on Western Channel ports, and 42 and 44 Flotillas based in the Bay of Biscay. Each flotilla was allocated up to twenty of these craft.

AUXILIARY SUBMARINE CHASERS (U-BOOTJAGEREN).
Fifteen in number allocated to 14 Flotilla and based on ports in the Bay of Biscay.

There were also a number of small patrol boats (VORPOSBOOTEN and KRIEGSFISCHKUTTEREN) divided between 2 Flotilla based on St Malo, 15 and 18 Flotillas based on Le Havre, and 4, 6 and 7 Flotillas based on ports in the Bay of Biscay.

GUN CARRIERS (ARTILLERIE-FAHREN), converted sea-going barges. There were forty-two of these vessels divided between 2 Flotilla in the area from Boulogne to Fécamp (31 craft) and 6 Flotilla in the area from Ouistreham to St Vaast (11 craft).

Some further sea-going barges (MARINE-FAHR-PRAHME) were fitted out and used for minelaying.

The estimated number of Kriegsmarine vessels in the area between Boulogne and Cherbourg available on 6th June varies according to source. Some estimate the figure as high as 125 whereas others put the number of craft of all types and sizes ready for sea-going service as low as 82.

When General Admiral Theodore Kranke commanding Naval Group Command West became aware of the Allied armada nearing the invasion beaches, orders were given to attack with three Torpedo Boats from Le Havre, the 6 Flotilla Gun Carriers stationed between Ouistreham and St Vaast to strike at the Allied landing craft, and for the Patrol Boats of 15 Flotilla at Le

Havre to reconnoiter the area. One of these Patrol Boats became the first German vessel to be lost in the operation. S-Boats of 5 and 9 Flotillas left Cherbourg but had to turn back because of heavy weather.

In the naval actions that followed D-Day and up to 13th June Kriegsmarine losses were as follows:

By ship-to-ship action - 4 Patrol Boats, 2 Destroyers, 2 Minesweepers, and 1 S-Boat.
By mines and air attacks - 2 Minesweepers, 5 S-Boats and 1 Gun Carrier.
Scuttling accounted for a further 6 vessels.

Kriegsmarine Torpedo Boats and S-Boats inflicted the following losses on Allied naval forces: 2 Destroyers (The Norwegian *Svenner* and USS *Nelson*), 4 landing ships, 3 landing craft, 3 Freighters, 1 Motor Torpedo Boat and 1 Tug.

XI THE LUFTWAFFE IN FRANCE

THIRD AIR FORCE (LUFTFLOTTE 3) with responsibilities covering France, Holland and Belgium, commanded by Generalfeldmarschall Hugo Sperrle with Headquarters in Paris.

Total available strength in early June 1944: about 950 aircraft.

FLIEGERKORPS II (II AIR CORPS)

Role: air support and tactical reconnaissance.
Strength in early June 1944: about 50 close support fighters under command of Generalleutenant Alfred Bulowins with Headquarters at Compiègne.

FLIEGERKORPS IX (IX AIR CORPS)

Role: minelaying and anti-shipping off-coast operations.
Strength: 130 bombers under command of Generalleutenant Dietrich Peltz with Headquarters at Beauvais.

FLIEGERKORPS X (X AIR CORPS)

Role: anti-shipping with missile-carrying bombers.
Strength in early June 1944: about 130 anti-shipping bombers plus 30 torpedo bombers with Division 2. Commanded by Generalleutenant Alexander Holle with Headquarters at Angers.

JADKORPS II (II FIGHTER CORPS)

Role: air defence.
Strength of Jagddivision 4: 71 day fighters, 29 night fighters.
Strength of Jagddivision 5: 29 day fighters. Commanded by Generalleutenant Werner Junck with Headquarters at Coulommiers and additional Headquarters at Bernay and Rennes.

In addition to the above Corps, Luftflotte 3 had a transport fleet of 31 serviceable aircraft in June 1944.

PRINCIPAL TYPES OF AIRCRAFT USED BY LUFTFLOTTE 3

Dornier 217: twin-engined bomber and night fighter.
Focke-Wulf 190: single-engined day fighter, also used for reconnaissance and ground attack.
Junkers 52: three-engined transport.
Junkers 88: twin-engined bomber, day and night fighter and reconnaissance aircraft.
Junkers 188: twin-engined bomber and long-range reconnaissance aircraft.
Messerschmidt 109: single-engined day and night fighter also used for reconnaissance.
Messerschmidt 110: twin-engined night fighter.
Messerschmidt 410: twin-engined bomber and reconnaissance aircraft.